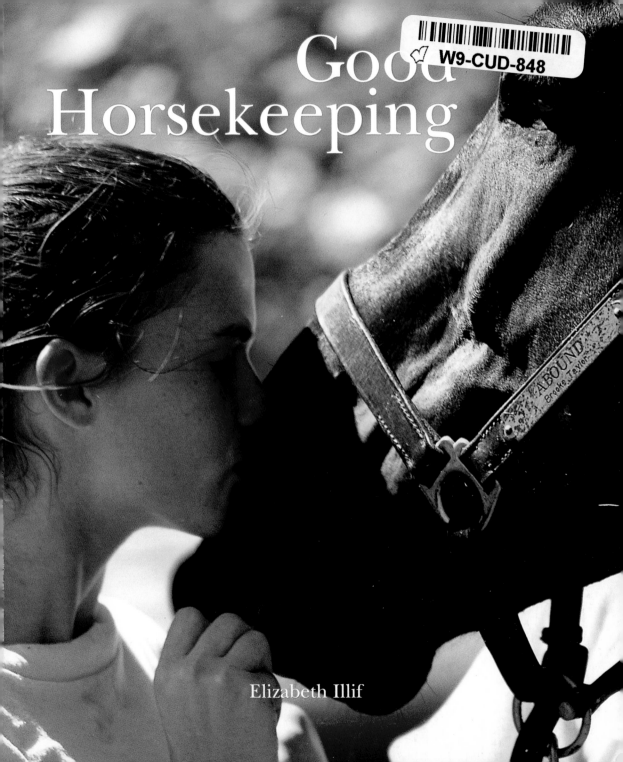

Good
Horsekeeping

Elizabeth Illif

A Note on Conventions Used in this Book

To avoid the awkward and impersonal nature of pronouns and phrases such as "one" and "his and/or her," I've chosen to refer to horses, farriers, and veterinarians as "he," and riders and riding instructors as "she" in most parts of the book. This is not meant to imply that there are no great female horses, farriers, or veterinarians, or male riders or instructors. Far from it! There are many of each. My apologies to members of the opposite sex in each case.

Good Horsekeeping

T.F.H. Publications, Inc.
One TFH Plaza
Third and Union Avenues
Neptune City, NJ 07753
www.tfhpublications.com

T.F.H. Publications
President/CEO: Glen S. Axelrod
Executive Vice president: Mark E. Johnson
Publisher: Christopher T. Reggio
Production Manager: Kathy Bontz

Project Team
Editor: Dominique DeVito
Copy Editor: Carl Shutt
Design: Mary Ann Kahn
Cover Design: Mary Ann Kahn

Library of Congress Cataloging-in-Publication Data
Iliff, Elizabeth.
Good horsekeeping : a comprehensive guide to all things equine / Elizabeth Iliff.
p. cm.
Includes bibliographical references.
ISBN 0-7938-2120-7 (alk. paper)
1. Horses. 2. Horses--Health. 3. Horsemanship. I. Title.
SF285.3.I45 2005
636.1—dc22
2005016376

Credits
Front and Back Cover Photos by Ed Camelli
TFH Archives: pp. 8, 16, 18 (top), 19, 29, 52, 53, 83, 114, 124, 125, 126, 127, 128, 130, 131, 140, 160, 225, 226
Erik Rudy: pp. 129
All Other Photos by Ed Camelli
Illustrations by Marta Samojeden

The Leader In Responsible Animal Care For Over 50 Years! ™
www.tfhpublications.com

"**E**xperts" in the horse world are a dime a dozen, but every now and then you come across someone whose knowledge and opinions are truly invaluable. In my 25-plus years of equine experience, I've been fortunate enough to meet quite a few truly expert horsemen and -women. To make this book as accurate and up-to-date as possible, I asked some of these professionals to review the chapters relevant to their expertise, which ranged from veterinary nutrition and medicine (both traditional and alternative) to stable management, entomology, shoeing, teaching theory, and animal behavior. Thanks to Baron Tayler, Sarah Ralston, Jerry Hogsette, Theo Schuff, Joyce Harman, Joni Werthan, Mary Ann Kean, Ann Grenci, Katie Phalen, Sue Louther, Jill Hassler-Scoop, Marcia Kulak, Linda Tellington-Jones, Bess Darrow, Ralph Hamor, and Mel and Barbara Dahl. Special thanks to Olympic veteran and coach Jim Wofford for taking the time to review the work in its entirety and share his ever-honest opinion of it.

Jill Lubing and the gals of Between the Covers book club generously gave their input from an amateur perspective. Dominique DeVito and the staff at TFH Publications were terrific for taking a chance on a first-time author and skillfully packaging my stacks of pages into a user-friendly book. Thanks to Jennifer Bryant for recommending me to Dominique and launching me into the world of publishing years ago, along with the help of Deb Lyons, whose terrific editorial skills rarely receive the recognition they deserve, and Ed Camelli, whose great photography illustrates this book.

My own background with horses has been enriched by too many people to list here. They include experts and amateurs, teachers and students, superstars and behind-the-scene volunteers. I'm equally grateful to my mentors and the people with whose methods I disagreed – for both challenged me to test and refine my own theories and techniques, thus deepening my understanding of horses.

Most importantly, thanks to my parents for supporting my equestrian pursuits over all of these years – and to the many wonderful horses who have taught me more than all of these humans put together.

Acknowledgements

Foreword

The world of horses has a mystique that newcomers often find confusing and even somewhat intimidating. I'm often approached by overwhelmed first-time horse owners anxiously asking: What sort of horse should I buy? Where shall I keep it? How do I know if my horse is sick? What sort of equipment will I need? The answers to all these questions—and many more—can be found in these pages.

Good Horsekeeping is the sort of book that every horse lover should have on their shelf. Not only will current horse owners find this guide useful, but anyone considering purchasing a horse now has an invaluable tool before taking that considerable step. Liz Iliff is one of those unusual authors who can take a complicated subject and make it simple. She is an excellent horsewoman and her knowledge of and feeling for these marvelous creatures shines through these pages. The reader can feel comfortable that they are getting good, solid advice, and the design of the book makes it easy to use as a reference guide.

With an abundance of important information available at your fingertips, *Good Horsekeeping* is a book all horse lovers will return to on a regular basis. You can be assured following the friendly, sound advice in this book will provide you with a healthy, safe, well-trained friend for life.

—James C. Wofford, a three-time Olympian, member of both the
United States Equestrian Association and the Culver Military Academy
Hall's of Fame, and one of the best-known Eventing trainers in the
world today. Wofford travels extensively, teaching and giving clinics.

Contents

Part 1

Welcome to the World of Horses

Chapter 1

So You Want to Ride a Horse?

Being involved with horses is not just a hobby—it's a lifestyle. Once you get into it, regardless of your other interests and responsibilities, most of your life gradually will begin to revolve around your horse. As an equine enthusiast, you already know how beautiful, charismatic, and intelligent these creatures are. But if you're planning on making the jump from horse lover to horse owner, there are a lot more things you need to know.

*Y*ou'll want to get familiar with equine behavior and learn what it takes to care for a horse: providing proper shelter, exercise, health care, and nutrition. This book will introduce you to the basics, but it's just the tip of the iceberg of all there is out there to learn about horses. Fortunately, there's no age limit in this sport—so take your time!

First: Get Help!

Learning to ride well is a lifelong endeavor. Even Olympic-level riders take regular lessons with their coaches. Because owning a horse involves so much responsibility, some people spend years riding schoolhorses (horses with a good temperament for teaching beginner riders) in lessons before buying a horse. The more you learn about riding and caring for horses properly, the better prepared you'll be to own your own.

You'll benefit most from an instructor who can provide you with a strong foundation of basic skills—proper balance and position in the saddle, use of the aids (your hands, legs and seat), etc. Like schoolteachers, the best riding instructors have infinite patience and compassion and a thorough knowledge of the subject being taught. Not all great instructors are naturally talented riders, however—and not all top-level riders are

Students who feel confident with their instructors will accomplish more.

good instructors. Judge a potential instructor on the accomplishments of her students, rather than on her own riding accomplishments.

Every instructor's top concern should be safety. Lessons should be challenging, but you should never feel like you're being pushed out of your comfort zone. Your instructor should have a good sense of what your horse is capable of doing, too, and should be able to get on him to demonstrate a skill or correct a behavior problem.

One of the best places to learn how to ride is in a reputable teaching facility that has a "string" of safe, experienced schoolhorses. Visit local barns and ask to watch a few lessons. Look for an instructor who shows empathy and understanding for both the horses and riders. Her students should appear confident and happy, not confused or scared. Just like any other professionals, instructors should have good credentials and references. Ask to speak to their other students and clients to get a feel for their methods and safety records.

Ownership Options

When you think you're ready to buy your first horse, sit down with your instructor to discuss your plans. This step is a biggie: you're going to need her judgment and guidance throughout the entire selection process. Rather than buying a horse straight off, ask her about partial-ownership opportunities. Some facilities organize horse-share programs that split one horse's expenses and riding availability among several riders. Another alternative is to lease a horse for the summer, the year, or even longer in a professional barn, where you can learn proper horse care from knowledgeable horse people. In some cases, lease deals can include an option to buy. These are all good ways

Finding an Instructor

Unfortunately, this country offers few certification programs for riding instructors, clinicians, and horse trainers. (Those programs that do exist are growing slowly, and they're setting good standards for equine professionals to aspire to and achieve.) You may have to rely on your own judgment and recommendations from friends when selecting an instructor. To locate ones in your area, ask the staff at your local tack shop for recommendations, consult organized equestrian groups (Pony Club, 4H, local riding clubs), and approach riders at local shows. Some national breed and discipline (specific sport) organizations also maintain lists of recommended instructors.

Everybody's an Expert

As you get more involved, you'll learn quickly that all horse people are experts—or at least they think they are. Because there are so many different riding and training methods out there, these "experts" will bombard you with varying—and sometimes completely contradictory—advice. This book will give you all the basic information you need to know about horses and will tell you how to find legitimate experts to consult with on more complicated issues. Choose professionals who always make safety and the horse's welfare their top priorities. Avoid working with "experts" who use methods that appear unsafe or inhumane.

to get your feet wet in the horse world without committing to the deep end.

Otherwise, your instructor may be able to arrange for you to buy or lease a schoolhorse or boarder's horse in the barn where you're taking lessons. If you trust that she has your best interests at heart (rather than her own financial interests), this can be an ideal opportunity.

Fitting a Horse into Your Life

Before welcoming this 1,000-pound animal into your life, ask yourself if you're ready to make certain sacrifices. Owning a horse is a major time and money commitment. If you keep him at home, you'll need to be there every day to feed, groom, exercise, and clean up after him. Balancing these responsibilities with a full-time job, family, or other hobbies can be overwhelming sometimes.

Even if you opt to board him at a full-care facility, you may find yourself spending hours each day grooming and exercising him. In either case, should your horse become ill or injured, you'll need to make extra time in your schedule to treat and care for him.

Let me make one thing clear from the beginning: there's no such thing as a cheap horse. Many first-time horse owners make the mistake of expecting the sale price of their new horse to be the biggest investment they'll make. Wrong! Compared to the boarding fees (or, if you're keeping your horse at home, the feed, hay, and maintenance expenses), veterinary bills, shoeing bills, and equipment purchases your horse will tally up for the next 10 to 15 years, his initial cost will be just a drop in the bucket. Price tags for suitable "first horses" range from about $2,000 to $50,000 or more. Once you've bought your horse, though, you may pay anywhere from $2,000 to

$20,000 a year for his regular care and maintenance. If you want to get involved competitively, the entry fees, stabling, and transportation costs could amount to hundreds—or even thousands—more.

One concern about horses that you should never underestimate is the element of risk involved. Horse-related accidents happen all the time, even to the best riders in the world. The sheer size and weight of a horse, combined with his natural instinct to move quickly when frightened or upset, make him an inherent danger to people on and around him. Even the gentlest, kindest horses can accidentally step on your foot, stumble and dislodge you from the saddle, or catch you by mistake with a kick aimed at another horse.

The more you know about equine behavior and the more realistic you are about your own riding abilities, the lower your risk of getting hurt. Also, as I'll explain later, your new horse's temperament will play a big role in your future safety—and in the safety of others. As a horse owner, you'll be responsible for any injuries your horse causes to others, whether accidentally or not. Children and pets, especially, can get underfoot easily and stepped on by a horse. If you allow them to play around your horse, their safety is in your hands.

'Til Death Do Us Part

Riders often keep their first horses for just two to three years. They either outgrow them literally (children growing too big for their ponies) or skill-wise (progressing beyond a horse's capabilities). When this happens, it's your responsibility to guarantee your horse a safe, healthy future. Horses can live to be 30 years or older, and many horses stay active and useful well into their later years. But

> **The Dirty Side**
>
> Don't let the neat, polished look you see in the horse-show ring fool you. Working with horses is a dirty business: mucking stalls, grooming muddy horses, cleaning sweaty tack, and doing loads and loads of smelly laundry. You'll never leave the barn clean—and slowly, without you even noticing it, your car and home will begin to take on the distinct aroma of horses. This may be perfume to a horse lover, but to non-horsey spouses, children, and roommates, it may signal the beginning of the end of a clean, happy household.

aging horses need a little extra TLC in the form of easily digestible foods and added protection from the elements. If you decide that your old friend no longer fits into your life, you owe it to him to find an acceptable new home where he'll receive the care he requires.

A shocking number of both young and old horses end up at horse auctions where meat dealers pick them up for low prices. Each year, tens of thousands of U.S. horses are shipped abroad or sent to two Texas-based slaughterhouses to be processed for human consumption in foreign countries. The terrifyingly brutal experience of slaughter is no way for any horse to end his life.

To be sure your beloved horse doesn't meet this end, incorporate a long-term plan into your original decision to purchase him. Ask yourself, "Do I have the resources to provide for him throughout his entire life, even if he's no longer useful to me or anyone else in his later years?"

If you decide to sell or give away your horse, no matter what his age, be sure his new owner guarantees in writing that he'll be well provided for and, when the time comes, humanely euthanized. If sending him to an auction is your only option, be sure to assign a reserve price to his sale that is higher than the current price of horsemeat.

After all of these cautions, you may be thinking, "Why would I want to own a horse?" Because the bond of understanding and friendship you'll form with him can become one of the most meaningful experiences in your life. You'll learn to communicate with this animal on so many different levels: physical, emotional, mental, and spiritual. Together, you may tackle the show ring, event course, trail . . . or maybe just your backyard. Regardless, partnering your humble human skills with the magnificent power, speed, and instincts of a horse

Part of the responsibility of being involved in horses is cleaning up after them.

will provide endless rewards. And, at the end of the day, you'll always have a warm, fuzzy neck to wrap your arms around!

Learn the Lingo

When you first spend time with horse people, they may seem to be communicating in a foreign language. Here are a few basic terms to help you keep up:

Age and Gender

Horses do the bulk of their growing in the first two years of life and then reach full size by age six or so. In many breeds and disciplines, however, they are considered mature at about age four. Because their teeth continue growing throughout life (the chewing motion grinds them down somewhat while they eat), the expression "long in the tooth" literally describes older horses. A veterinarian or equine dentist can estimate a horse's age simply by looking at his teeth. Here's how we describe horses of different ages:

foal – baby horse less than one year old

filly – female foal

colt – male foal

weanling – foal who has been weaned (taken away) from his or her

Before you get involved with horses, be sure you're prepared to accept the risks involved.

Here, a mare and foal are exercising in a paddock. The world of horses has its own vocabulary, too.

mother, usually at about four to six months of age

yearling, two-year-old, three-year-old – just like they sound (Note: In some breeds, such as the Thoroughbred, every horse is considered a year older on January 1st, regardless of his or her actual birthday.)

mare – mature female

stallion – mature male

gelding – castrated male

dam – mother

sire – father

Body Parts

Some names of horse parts are pretty self-explanatory: eyes, head, neck, back, and so on. To familiarize yourself with other key parts, review the diagram on page 17 and refer to it throughout the book.

The Equine Rainbow

Believe it or not, there are red, blue, and green horses. (A green horse is not actually the color green—unless he just rolled in the pasture and has grass stains. In horse lingo, "green" means inexperienced or lacking training.) There are also many special words used to describe different

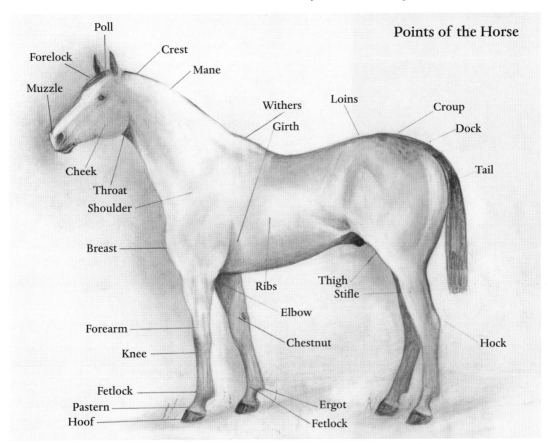

Points of the Horse

Poll
Crest
Forelock
Mane
Muzzle
Withers
Loins
Croup
Girth
Dock
Cheek
Tail
Throat
Shoulder
Breast
Thigh
Stifle
Ribs
Elbow
Forearm
Chestnut
Hock
Knee
Fetlock
Pastern
Ergot
Hoof
Fetlock

shades within each color, as well as rare and unusual colors. These may vary somewhat from breed to breed. To get by in the horse world, you'll need to know these basic terms:

points – a horse's mane and tail and, in some cases, lower legs. Looking at a horse's points helps you determine what color he is.

bay – reddish to dark brown body, with black points.

black – black body, points, and muzzle (Many people mistake a dark-bay horse for black. The best way to determine a horse's true color is to look closely at the hairs on his muzzle.)

chestnut (or sorrel) – copperish-brown body with matching mane and tail.

gray – black and white hairs mixed together, or just white hairs. Most grays

This horse's reddish-brown color and black mane mean he's a true bay.

The copper color of this horse's coat and mane mark him as a chestnut.

are darker colored at birth. They may become dappled (covered with a pattern of dark circular markings) or steel gray as they mature, then eventually turn white. Older horses may develop small brown spots on their coats, which label them as "flea-bitten" grays. Most white horses are actually older grays. To be truly white, a horse must have a pink muzzle, light-colored hooves, and no colored hairs.

roan – white hairs mixed in with a solid color. Unlike grays, roans maintain the colored hairs in their heads and lower legs throughout life. A black, or "blue," roan has white hairs mixed with black. A chestnut, or "red," roan has copperish-brown hairs mixed with white. A "strawberry" roan has black and reddish hairs mixed with white.

buckskin (or dun) – yellowish-gray or golden body with black mane and tail.

palomino – yellowish or golden body with white mane and tail.

Pinto (or Paint) – mixture of white and large black or colored spots or patches. The Pinto is actually a breed of horse as well as a color. Similar color patterns are also characteristic of most horses in the Paint Horse breed. Many special terms are used to describe these horses' different possible patterns of spots and markings.

Appaloosa – also both a color and a breed, characterized by colored spots distributed over the body (a leopard pattern) or over an area of white on the horse's rump (a blanket pattern).

If you hear of more obscure colors like *grullo, overo, tobiano, tovero, perlino,* and *cremello,* don't be afraid to ask someone to point them out. Many experienced horse people don't even know what they look like!

Marks of Distinction

Besides their coat colors and personalities—which vary as much as human personalities—horses can be distinguished from one another by the markings on their faces and legs. Not all horses have markings (because markings are so common, though, being "unmarked" is an equally distinctive characteristic), but when they do, they're usually uniquely—and memorably—placed.

How Does He Measure Up?

The height of a horse is measured in "hands." Each hand is four inches. A 15.2-hand ("fifteen-two hand") horse, for example, is 15 hands plus two inches, which works out to 62 inches tall. A horse is measured at the highest point of his withers, the bony curve between his neck and back. Technically, any horse 14.2 hands or smaller is called a pony; any bigger than 14.2 is called a horse—regardless of breed. (Note: Laypeople commonly confuse ponies with foals. The term "pony" has nothing to do with an animal's age. It merely means that he's not taller than 14.2 hands. As I'll explain later, "pony breeds" are known for producing animals below this height limit.) The average horse stands about 15.2 to 16.2 hands tall, but some larger breeds can grow to 18 hands or higher!

Right, Left, . . . Right?

With four legs rather than two, horses have more ways of natural locomotion to choose from than humans do. We call the particular patterns in which they move their legs "gaits." Most horses have four basic gaits:

walk – this is the slowest of the gaits. Each leg moves individually, creating a four-beat rhythm.

trot (or jog) – the legs move in diagonal pairs, creating

These two horses may look like different colors but they're both considered "gray."

Some breeds, such as Friesians and Clydesdales, have long hairs on their lower legs, called "feathers."

19

The colored spots all over this pony make it clear to all that he is an appaloosa.

The average horse weighs between about 900 and 1,200 pounds. So stay clear of dancing hooves! Being stepped on by a 1,000-pound animal is no laughing matter.

a two-beat rhythm. Between each beat, there is a "moment of suspension" when all four legs are off the ground.

canter (or lope) – in this three-beat gait, the horse steps with one hind leg, then steps simultaneously with the other hind leg and its diagonal front leg, then finally pushes off with the remaining front leg. A moment of suspension follows before the original hind leg touches the ground again. When cantering, a horse appears to lead with the foreleg that leaves the ground last before the moment of suspension. Depending on which leg appears to be leading, he's said to be cantering on his "right lead" or "left lead."

gallop – the fastest of the gaits, this looks like a sped-up canter, except that each leg strikes the ground independently, creating a distinct four-beat rhythm.

The legendary racehorse Man o' War pushed so hard off the ground when he galloped that he covered 28 feet with each stride!

Other gaits – some breeds, such as Standardbreds, Saddlebreds, and Paso Finos, have a few extra gaits in their repertoire. The pace, running walk, slow gait, and rack look and feel completely different from the basic four gaits.

Other Need-to-Know Terms

tack – what the horse wears when you ride him (saddle, bridle, etc.).

halter – fits around a horse's head and attaches to a lead shank (like a dog leash), with which you lead him around.

stall – a horse's private "bedroom" in the stable.

turn-out – outdoor playtime, when a horse is allowed to move around and get some fresh air in an enclosed area, called a paddock, corral, or pasture.

mucking – removing manure and soiled bedding from a horse's stall. (Not only is this pastime mentally satisfying—every day you transform a smelly, messy stall into a clean, fresh one—but it's also an excellent upper-body workout.)

lame – limping with one or more legs because of discomfort caused by an injury, ailment, or shoeing problem.

sound – the opposite of lame. A horse's history of "soundness" is a crucial factor in determining his potential as a useful mount for your purposes. A "serviceably sound" horse may have minor leg or hoof problems, but is still able to do the job you ask him to do with proper veterinary and shoeing maintenance.

Prophet's Thumbprint

See a thumbprint-sized indentation on your horse's chest or the underside of his neck? Some people consider this "prophet's thumbprint" a sign of good luck. It's actually a fairly common old muscle injury caused by a kick from another horse or by running into a fence. Because there's no bone directly underneath the surface in this area, the skin usually isn't broken by the injury. Only the underlying muscle fibers are affected. The impact splits and breaks the fibers, leaving a permanent indentation

Chapter 2

Understanding Horses

The best way to understand horses is to try to see the world through their eyes. Their instincts, senses, and social structures are different from ours, so their needs and reactions to various situations are different, too. The more we study them, the better we can predict their behavior, and the more easily we can communicate our needs to them. We don't know everything about equine nature yet—not by a long shot—but this chapter will review what we do know.

Equine Senses

Because horses evolved as prey animals, their senses are finely tuned to respond quickly to the approach of potential predators. They're constantly processing information, ever ready to react to any sudden changes in their surroundings.

Vision

In most situations, horses see much better than we do. Because their eyes are positioned on the sides of their heads, rather than in front like ours, they see most things with one eye—called monocular vision—rather than with two eyes—binocular vision. That's why horses often shy away from an object when approaching it from one direction, even if they've already seen it from the other direction. Seen with the other eye, the object looks entirely new again. So, when you walk a horse past something spooky (something he'd consider suspicious), do it from both directions so he can register the information through both eyes.

The most impressive quality of a horse's eyesight is his peripheral vision. He has an almost 360-degree view of the world around him. However, he does have one blind spot directly in front of his muzzle and one behind him. To avoid startling a horse, never approach him from directly in front or behind his body.

The shaded areas in front of the horse's head and behind it are his blind spots.

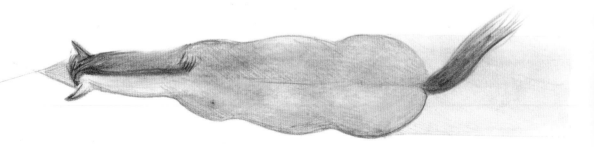

One of the ways horses focus their eyes on objects is by changing their head position. To see faraway things better, they raise their heads. To see closer things, they lower them. When a horse approaches a jump, for example, he'll first raise his head to locate it from a distance. Then, as he gets closer, he'll gradually lower his head. (Note: Because of the blind spot in front of his nose, the jump disappears entirely from his field of view just before he leaves the ground. That's why it's so important for him to focus on it and register its dimensions in his brain ahead of time so he can safely clear it.)

Our four-legged friends also have exceptional night vision. However, their eyes adjust slowly when going suddenly from light to dark. This is why, for example, some

As far as we know, horses can see some colors: red, blue, and possibly yellow and green.

Horses raise or lower their heads to help them see objects more clearly. The raised heads on this group indicate they're looking at something far away from them.

Everybody Poops

Depending on a horse's diet, exercise, and the weather conditions, he may urinate and defecate as infrequently as two or three times a day or as often as once every two to three hours. Stallions use urination and defecation as a way to mark territory. Chemical messengers, called pheromones, in urine and manure tell other horses, "I was here!" So don't be surprised when your mount pauses on a trail ride to sniff a pile of manure. He's just checking to see whose calling card it is.

event horses and foxhunters are hesitant to jump obstacles going from a sunny field into a shadowy forest.

A good way to figure out what a horse is focusing his eyes on is by watching his ears. Usually, when he pricks both ears straight ahead, he's also focusing both eyes in that direction.

Hearing

Horses' large, cuplike ears are built to swivel independently of each other, zeroing in on sound waves like rotating satellite dishes. Because they've evolved to detect subtle snaps and rustling of twigs and grass made by approaching predators, horses can hear a much wider range of high-frequency sounds than we can.

The most important thing to know about a horse's sense of hearing is that it's hard-wired to his emotions. Unexpected or unfamiliar sounds can evoke an instant fear reaction in a horse, causing him to spook (startle and jump or run away from the noise) suddenly. Some horses are more emotionally reactive than others—and most react more dramatically than usual when they're in an unfamiliar environment, such as a horse show.

When you're leading, grooming, or riding a horse, watch which way he turns the open, cupped parts of his ears. If he swivels one or both toward an object that he may perceive as scary or foreign, immediately try to direct his attention elsewhere. If you react quickly enough, you may avert a spook. (Chapter 3 will discuss what other ear positions mean in equine body language.)

When you approach a horse, take advantage of his sensitive hearing. Speak in a soft voice to let him know you're coming and to avoid startling him. If one or both of his ears swivel in your direction, he knows you're there.

Smell

The equine sense of smell is also much more sensitive than our own. A horse's large nostrils constantly draw in scents from the environment. Within his long nasal passages, millions of nerve cells, called olfactory receptors, analyze the smells and send messages to his brain for processing. A second set of smell sensors, called the vomeronasal organs, detect and analyze pheromones, the chemical signals released into the air by other animals. Pheromones are closely linked to the endocrine (hormone) system. For example, a mare's pheromones can tell a stallion when she is in heat (ready to be bred).

Horses use their sense of smell for finding food and water and to identify approaching predators, as well as for interacting with each other socially. A mare will lick and smell her newborn baby thoroughly to memorize his unique scent. When new horses meet each other, they breathe deeply into each other's noses, using their personal odors to introduce themselves. Horses may "sniff you out," too, gently blowing on your hands and body and breathing in your smell. When you approach

Horses have large nostrils and long nasal passages, making their sense of smell much more sensitive than ours. They use it for identification and communication.

When horses get a whiff of something especially pungent, they will raise their head and curl their upper lip in what is called the Flehmen Response.

The Flehmen Response

You might wonder if a horse just heard a funny joke when you see him raise his head and curl his upper lip into the air, doing what's known as the "Flehmen" response. What he's really doing is trapping a smell in his nasal passages, allowing his vomeronasal organs more time to analyze them. Flehmen responses are triggered primarily by sex pheromones, but they can also be stimulated by unusually strong or pungent odors.

any horse, give him a moment to smell you, standing quietly or slowly offering your hand for inspection.

Touch

Here's one of the contradictions in horses: Although they have strong hides that seem to tolerate heavy blows, kicks, and bites from other horses, their skin is extremely sensitive to the lightest touch of a fly. The same goes for their responsiveness to riders. Horses are capable of sensing very light touches of our legs on their sides or gentle pressure on the bits in their mouths; however, some can become so desensitized to these aids that they only respond to firm kicks and tugs on the bridle. It's our job as riders, therefore, to avoid overusing or misusing our aids in such a way that desensitizes horses to them.

Do you know how you can move the skin in your forehead to raise your eyebrows? Horses can do that almost anywhere on their bodies. When a fly lands on a horse's back, for example, he can vibrate a localized area of skin underneath the fly, and try to shake it off. You might see a section of a horse's coat quiver similarly in response to something ticklish or irritating while you're grooming him, for instance.

Fight or Flight

One instinct that has remained fairly strong in horses over the centuries is the fight-or-flight response. In the wild, when threatened by a predator, horses usually choose to flee rather than fight. However, given no option to run, they will resort to using their teeth and hooves to defend themselves and their families.

Domestic horses usually choose flight over fight, too, unless they're cornered. When treated fairly and patiently,

One of the most sensitive parts of the horse is his muzzle. He uses it to touch and explore new things in his environment and to seek out the most appealing morsels in his hay, grain, and pasture.

This horse's raised head, alert ears, wide nostrils, raised tail, and cantering movement are "flight" responses to something that has surprised or scared him.

Here's a common myth about horses: "They can't sleep lying down." It's true that horses can sleep standing up, thanks to a mechanism in their legs that locks in place as they doze off. But they also do sleep lying down—sometimes flat out on their sides with their heads and necks outstretched—as frequently as several times a day. When pastured in groups, horses tend to rest at the same time, while an individual remains standing on guard. Some horses even "run" in their sleep, twitching their legs as if they were racing. Scientists believe that these episodes may correspond to deep or rapid eye movement (REM) sleep.

they rarely resort to aggressive behavior toward humans. Their flight instinct may show through now and then in the form of a spook, shy, or bolt (these are all commonly used terms for the same flight reaction). This "run first, ask questions later" reaction is completely natural, but it can be trained out of most horses. One who trusts his rider and handlers can learn to stay focused on his job without shying away from even the most disturbing surprises, such as fireworks and honking horns. The calm, steady police mounts patrolling the busy streets of New York City are a perfect example.

Always assume that any quick motions, loud noises, or strange objects may spook a horse, especially one unfamiliar to you. Never run or yell around the stableyard. When you're near a horse, beware of things that may set him off (bicycles, car horns, tarps, umbrellas, balloons, flags, pets, small children, wildlife, etc.). Keep an eye on him and maintain a safe distance between you whenever you're not sure how he'll react.

Built to Graze and Roam

Horses are essentially lawn mowers. In the wild, they spend 60 to 80 percent of their time munching on grass, leaves, herbs, and other vegetation. Their digestive systems evolved to be very different from ours. Instead of eating a few large meals per day, they're designed to take in small amounts of food throughout the day and night. As I'll explain in Chapter 18, the healthiest diet for a domestic horse consists of small, frequent, high-roughage meals.

Because it takes so much exploring to find a day's worth of food, horses also evolved to be almost constantly on the move. In the wild, they may travel many miles per day to find good grazing, water, and rest sites. Although domestic horses learn to adapt to more confined spaces, regular exercise and access to open spaces are still critical to their physical and mental health.

Herd Behavior

In the wild, horses live in large herds made up of several smaller "harem bands." Each harem band usually consists of one mature stallion, several mature mares, and their young offspring. Although the stallion is responsible for defending the herd against intruders, the actual harem leader is usually a mature mare. She makes the decisions to move to new grazing areas, trek to water, and settle down to rest.

Contrary to popular belief, horses don't interact in a linear social hierarchy, where horse A is dominant over horse B, horse B is dominant over horse C, and so on. The dominant and submissive roles among herd members are more complex and interchangeable, depending on various circumstances. For example, one horse may be submissive to another when

Horses are herd animals who, in the wild, establish social order over time.

they're alone together, but dominant to the same animal when he's with a companion. Horses can have "triangular" relationships, too. For instance, horse A may be dominant over horse B, horse B may be dominant over horse C, but then horse C may be dominant over horse A. An individual horse's role in the herd can change throughout his lifetime, as well. As he matures, he may become dominant over a horse to whom he was submissive as a youngster.

Because the social order within each band evolves gradually over time, and may even be passed down from one generation to the next, seriously aggressive behavior is rare in the wild. Closely matched pairs of horses, such as young bachelor stallions, often spar with one another, but most herd interactions are peaceful and nonaggressive. Domestic horses are a different story. By confining groups of unrelated, unfamiliar horses in fenced areas, we disturb their natural social structure. With less time and space to establish their dominance relationships, some domestic horses resort to unnaturally aggressive behavior, often injuring their pasturemates. It's very important, therefore, to introduce new horses to one another gradually—stabling them next to each other or putting them in adjoining paddocks before letting them loose in a pasture together—and then observe their initial interactions carefully.

As natural herd animals, horses prefer to live in the company of others. Keeping a horse alone may be emotionally stressful for him, causing him to fret, lose weight, and develop behavior problems. If he has just one buddy, his herd instinct may bond him so closely to the other horse that they'll become practically inseparable. This can make any brief separations (taking one horse away for a ride, clinic, etc.) traumatic for one or both of them.

> In most situations, it's easiest to keep horses in groups of three or more—either together in a pasture or within view of each other in separate stalls or paddocks. Horses are usually happier exercising in the company of others, too.

The Alpha-Leader Myth

Many horse people describe specific horses as "alpha mares" or "alpha leaders." In wild horse bands, such an individual rarely exists. Leadership and defense roles are played by a number of different horses within a band. In domestic situations, however, introduction of a highly desirable, limited resource—such as grain—can cause more competition within groups of horses. A single individual may use overt aggression to try to control the resource (i.e., chase other horses away from grain buckets and feeders), showing dominance in this particular situation. However, he or she may not necessarily take on all of the other leadership roles of the herd—choosing grazing sites, defending against intruders, etc. So, even in the unnatural conditions we create for our horses, there still aren't true "alpha leaders."

Trying to take on an "alpha" role with a horse, therefore, may not be the best approach to forming a strong relationship with him. You may need to mimic dominant body language to earn his respect now and then, but beware of using too much force with him when he's exhibiting submissive behavior. Try to establish a relationship in which neither of you takes advantage of (or risks hurting) the other, yet both of you are willing to cooperate and work together.

Keeping a horse alone may be emotionally stressful for him.

Chapter 3

Horse-Handling Basics

Great horsemanship is a combination of good instincts, precise body control, and an excellent understanding of equine behavior and communication. To the untrained eye, effective communication with horses may seem magical. It's not. Even a city slicker can learn to recognize basic equine facial expressions and body movements—and then, with practice, use that knowledge to anticipate and influence a horse's actions. From the moment he arrives at his new home, begin working on building a relationship with your horse. Use your voice, body language, and basic handling skills to guide him, to establish limits—and to ensure both his and your safety.

Equine Communication

First, since a horse can't speak English (or any other human language), you need to learn his language. Horses use a complex vocabulary of head gestures, body movements, and vocal sounds to communicate with one another. The position of a horse's ears is especially telling: pricked forward, they're generally signaling alertness, curiosity, or interest. Slightly flopped to the sides, they indicate relaxation, sleep, or boredom. If they're rotated backward, he's listening to something behind him. However, if they're rotated backward and flattened down against his neck, they're indicating fear or anger. The direction in which the ears point usually indicates where a horse's attention is focused. Ideally, when you're working with him, he should always have at least one ear cocked in your direction, listening for your next cue.

Although horses can't learn to speak our words, they can learn to recognize and respond to some of them. For example, "whoa" is a common word used to tell horses to stop or slow down. Many horses are trained to respond to "walk," "trot," and "canter," too. When using voice commands, the tone of your voice is as important as the words you use. Many people start with a low note and then lift to a higher note at the end of the command to indicate that they want the horse to increase speed: "trrr-OT!" To slow down, they do the opposite, ending on a lower, more soothing note: "TR-ooot." In general, horses respond better to calm, clear, low voices rather than excited screeches. (That's why you'll occasionally see a runaway horse accelerate when his rider starts desperately screaming, "Whoa! Whoa!") Consistency is key: Try to use the same word and tone of voice for every command every time you use it.

Horses use a wide variety of sounds to communicate. The loud, prolonged whinny, or neigh, is most often used as a friendly greeting between a pair of familiar horses as they approach each other. A nicker is a low-pitched, guttural, pulsating sound that mares and foals use with each other—and that a horse might use to greet you (especially at feeding time). Squeals, screams, grunts, and snorts are used during mock and serious fighting. Horses also groan sometimes when they lie down or when they're physically uncomfortable. When faced with something foreign or frightening, they may "blow" with a strong, sharp exhalation. This loud noise apparently communicates alarm to other herd members. Your mount might do it when you encounter strange objects or animals on trail rides or in other unfamiliar circumstances.

Body Language

Besides his facial gestures and vocalizations, a horse will communicate with you and other horses and animals with various body postures. In general, if he turns to face you, with his ears pricked, he's in a friendly mood. If he turns his tail toward you or walks away, he probably doesn't want to have anything to do with you. There's a wide range of behavior in between that you'll gradually pick up as you spend more time with him.

Horses rarely bite or kick without warning. They'll usually threaten an offending horse or human first with flattened ears and perhaps a bluff kick

This pony's body language shows that he's relaxed and trusting despite the busyness around him. Notice the nearly closed eyes and ears drooping to the sides.

or snapping teeth not intended to make contact. In response, submissive horses usually retreat a safe distance away. Youngsters, in particular, may demonstrate a submissive posture: opening and closing the jaw, lowering the head in a nursing posture, and lowering the body by bending the knees and hunching the hindquarters.

To avoid getting hurt, always watch for signs of disgruntled or aggressive behavior. For example, if you walk past a horse's stall and he flattens his ears and bares his teeth, step out of his reach. Once you've gotten more comfortable reading body language, you'll know when it's safe to imitate more dominant behavior—standing tall, squaring your shoulders, and using a firm, low voice—to show a horse that you are his social equal. Remember that horses are much bigger and stronger than you. Never risk your own body trying to "subdue" or "face down" an aggressive or dangerous horse. Leave those challenges to the experts.

Give Me Space!

To earn a horse's respect—and, more importantly, to ensure your safety—you must establish the boundaries of your personal space. Imagine a 6- to 12-inch bubble of air around you and make it clear that it's never okay for him to break that bubble. If he steps into it with a foot, leans in with a shoulder, or nudges in with his nose, firmly say, "No!" and press him back out of your space. Most horses will respond to a gentle poke with the fingers or elbow. If you get no response, add more pressure and push his lead rope away from you. If that still doesn't work (and some spoiled horses can be very pushy), carry a short whip or crop and tap him on the shoulder with the blunt end whenever he invades your space. Only use as much force as is necessary. You should be able to decrease the amount of force as he learns what you want. If he doesn't improve, ask an expert for help.

Maintaining your space is important in everything you do around a horse. When you're grooming him, for example, teach him to step his hindquarters away from you in response to a gentle prod on his side (at the spot where your leg would be if you were in the saddle). This will make it easier to work around him and will prevent him from crowding you dangerously against walls and fences.

Giving treats is an easy way to encourage a horse unintentionally to intrude in your space. When you do offer him a treat, if he gets pushy—shoves you with his nose or tramples on your toes—gently push him back and deny him the treat. (Giving the treat at that point would just reward and encourage the bad behavior.) Wait until he patiently stands outside your space before saying, "Good boy," and giving him the treat.

Approaching a Horse

The most important thing to do whenever approaching a horse is to let him know where you are. Horses startle easily, particularly if someone sneaks up in their blind spots (behind or directly in front of them). Never approach a

Horses and people need to be respectful of each others' space so that neither of you crowds the other, which can lead to defensive and potentially dangerous behavior.

One of the things you'll hear many horse people say is: "Show him who's boss!" This is an old-fashioned—and slightly outdated—saying. No, you don't want to let a horse boss you around—that could be dangerous. But your relationship will be much more rewarding and successful if you think of yourselves as partners, rather than boss and servant. You do want his respect and obedience, but it's usually not necessary to intimidate a horse to the point of absolute submission (the extreme of which is often described as a "broken spirit"). And it's never okay to be abusive. As an old horse adage says, "Where abuse begins, learning ends."

horse from directly behind him. Even the nicest horse may kick out in surprise. Instead, talk or hum quietly as you approach his shoulder at an angle. If he's in a stall and has his tail turned to you, make a clucking noise to him with your tongue or shake a bucket of grain to encourage him to turn around. Then, slowly reach your hand out and rub his shoulder.

In the pasture, it's easier to have horses come to you than to trek out to them. Many learn to recognize a whistle or special call (some even come to their names). If you do have to approach a horse in the middle of a pasture, follow the same advice described above: let him know you're coming before walking toward his shoulder. A treat or bucket of grain is always great incentive for a horse to come in from the pasture. (If you use grain, feed it sparingly. Too much grain can be unhealthy for some horses.)

However, if he's turned out with other horses, be prepared to be surrounded by hungry, pushy noses. Competition for treats can create skirmishes that you don't want to get caught in the middle of. So, it's best if a horse learns to come to you alone, and then receive the treat when the other horses aren't looking—or after you've taken him out of the pasture.

Haltering

As you're getting to know a horse, put a halter on him every time you interact. This will give you a certain amount of control over him, allowing you to position his body safely around yours at all times. For example, it's not an uncommon equine behavior, particularly in young or temperamental horses, for a horse to wheel around and kick out with his hind legs at someone or something. By keeping a hold of his head with the halter, you can keep

yourself near the "safe" end. Once you're more familiar with his habits and personality, you'll be able to do more work around him without a halter.

When catching your horse in the pasture, teach him to come to you. Luring him with a treat is helpful.

Unless you're dealing with a horse who is especially sensitive about having his ears touched, it's usually easiest to learn how to use a halter that has a snap on the throatlatch (the part on the side of the horse's jaw), so you can leave the crownpiece (the part that goes behind his ears) attached. To put the halter on, approach the horse's left ("near") shoulder and rub him gently on the neck. Slowly slip the lead rope around his neck to keep him from stepping away. Holding the crownpiece of the halter in your right hand and the noseband in your left hand, guide it slowly over his nose. Then bend his ears forward, one ear at a time, with your right hand, while lifting the crownpiece of the halter over them with your left. Snap the throatlatch in place.

Next, check to be sure the halter fits properly. The noseband should rest about two fingers' widths below his cheekbone. You should be able to fit two fingers between the noseband and his nose and two fingers between his jawbone and the throatlatch. The halter should fit clear of both eyes and shouldn't hang loosely enough that he could catch a hoof in it.

It's easiest to have the lead rope already attached to the halter when you put it on. For most purposes, you'll want it connected to the lowest ring or loop centered under the horse's chin. Using the upper side ring may cause the halter to shift and pinch his eye on the opposite side.

Leading

You can lead a horse from either side—and it's good to teach horses to be lead from both sides—but the traditional side to lead from is the horse's left, or "near" side. (His right side is the "far" side.) Hold the lead rope in your right hand, thumb facing up, about 5 to 6 inches from the halter. Hold the remaining rope folded up in your left hand. If the horse is wearing a bridle, take the reins over his neck so you can hold both of them in your right hand several inches below his chin. Double the excess back and forth and hold it in your left hand. Never wrap the lead rope or reins in a loop around your hand—this can cause serious accidents if the horse suddenly spooks or tries to break free.

There's a difference between "leading" a horse and "dragging" a horse. Like a well-trained dog "heeling" at his master's side, a horse should walk willingly next to you, with his shoulders about even with your shoulders and with the lead rope slack. He shouldn't barge ahead, pulling on the rope, or lag behind. If he gets ahead of you, give a firm yank on the rope and say, "Whoa!" As soon as he slows down, relax the pressure on the rope again to reward him. If he lags behind, cluck to him with your tongue, or say "Walk on!" encouragingly, while gently tugging the rope forward and giving him slack again when he catches up.

To turn a horse to the right, move the lead rope under his chin to the right, moving his head away from you. If he doesn't respond to this, give his neck a nudge with your elbow or knuckles. To turn left, simply turn your own body left and use gentle pressure on the rope to ask him to follow. Never allow him to crowd or lean on you. If he moves into your space, poke his neck with your elbow or knuckles and turn his head toward you with the lead rope so his neck and shoulder bend away from

you. If he habitually crowds you, carry a whip in one hand and tap it on his shoulder or neck whenever he gets too close.

Lead Carefully

Be careful leading a horse past things that might spook him—barking dogs, lawnmowers, etc. Be sure he's walking obediently alongside and paying attention to you. Try to put yourself between him and the scary object as you walk past it, to avoid having him jump away from it—and on top of you. Use a calm, encouraging voice and gentle pressure on the lead rope if he tries to race away. Once you're safely past, praise him and stroke him on the neck.

Also take special care whenever leading a horse through tight openings, such as gates and stall doorways. Remember, he has a long body that's not always easy to maneuver in confined spaces. Be sure he has plenty of room on both sides before walking him through the opening, then

The traditional way to lead a horse is to be on his left side and hold the lead rope with your right hand. Using a properly attached chain shank, as demonstrated here, can give you added control.

continue walking straight until his tail is through the opening before asking him to turn around. (Hip injuries are commonly caused by negligent handlers who turn horses too suddenly as they're entering their stalls, causing the horses to slam a hip into the wall.) When you lead a horse into a pasture, always turn him to face the gate, and then close it securely before letting him go.

Be careful whenever leading a horse near other horses, too. Just because they have humans attached to the other ends of their lead lines doesn't mean they won't interact with each other in a "horsey" manner. An ill-placed kick, strike, or bite could be tragic for both horses and humans. So always keep several horses' widths between your horse and others.

Tying

There are basically two ways to tie a horse: with a single rope or with two "crossties." (Crossties are ropes or straps hung from opposite sides of an aisle or stall. They attach to either side of a horse's halter, limiting his head movement from side to side. Some people prefer to use crossties for grooming, tacking up, etc.) Here are a few important tying tips:

★ The best rule of thumb: If you can't find a safe place to tie a horse, don't tie him. Always tie to something solid and secure, such as a thick, well-seated post that won't break free if he pulls hard backward. Many accidents result from horses tied to flimsy objects (gates, fence poles, etc.), which then break off when they pull back and crash around their legs as they run away. Also, never tie a horse where he might step on or bump into dangerous objects.

★ Attach a breakable piece of twine to your tie ring or post. Tie the horse's lead rope to this, rather than directly to the ring or post. The twine should break under pressure before the halter or lead rope does. So, if the horse breaks free, he'll still have an intact halter and lead rope on—making him much easier to catch. Tie homemade crossties to similar breakaway attachments or, if you purchase commercially made crossties, select ones designed with a safety-release feature. Check that the quick-release feature is attached to the wall or post—not to the end of the tie that attaches to the horse's halter.

★ Use a quick-release knot.

★ Tie the horse to something that is his shoulder height or higher, loosely enough so he can relax his head and neck, but not so loosely that he might reach a hoof over the lead rope.

★ If a horse does panic and pull back when he's tied, back out of his way so you don't get trampled. Speak in a soothing, quiet voice to try to calm him. If you can reach the quick-release knot without endangering yourself, step in and pull it free. Otherwise, wait until he's stopped struggling before trying to approach him.

★ Before crosstying a horse who is new to you, ask his former owner if he's been crosstied before. The added restriction of movement can make some horses nervous. To make it most comfortable for the horse, connect the crossties to the side rings of his halter and adjust them to a length that allows him to lower his head to about chest level and to move it slightly side to side. The best crosstie locations are in stalls or grooming stalls with solid back walls—so, if a horse panics and tries to run backward, he'll just bump into the wall and, hopefully, step back into the proper position.

Tying a Quick-Release Knot

If a horse is tied up with a proper quick-release knot, you should be able to simply pull on the loose end to set him free. Here's how to tie it:

★ Run the lead rope through a tie ring or around a secure post.

★ Cross the loose end of the rope over the part connected to the horse's halter.

★ Make a loop out of the loose end, folding it back over itself.

★ Holding the first loop in place, make a second loop out of the remaining part of the rope.

★ Bring this loop around under the attached rope and then through the first loop, pulling it until the knot closes snugly.

★ Check the length of the tie and redo the knot if necessary.

★ The horse should have enough freedom to move his head and neck, but not so much that he can reach a foot over the rope.

★ Whenever a horse is tied, try not to do anything that might startle or scare him. For example, if someone needs to start up a loud engine—a lawnmower, leaf blower, etc.—ask them to do it a safe distance from the horse. If you're worried that the horse still might react to the noise, untie him completely and hold him by hand.

Self-Grooming

No matter how thoroughly you brush and curry a horse, he'll probably still resort to some of his own grooming techniques—or appeal to a buddy to help him out. Horses love to roll on their backs, usually in a nice, dusty area that's been established by repeated use. To relieve an itch or loosen shedding hair, they'll rub their heads and bodies against trees, fences, and even fellow pasturemates.

Horses love to roll on their backs.

Mutual grooming is a popular bonding activity for horses, as well as a good way to aid in shedding, parasite control, and stress relief. Two horses will stand beside one another, usually facing head-to-tail or head-to-shoulder, using their muzzles and teeth to gently nip, nuzzle, or rub each other's neck and withers. Try scratching a horse with your knuckles in these areas, watching the reaction in his face. When you've hit "the spot," he'll stick his upper lip out to show his pleasure, and may even reach around to nuzzle your shoulder ("you scratch my back, I'll scratch yours"). Gently push his nose away to discourage him from nipping, so he learns to accept this attention without feeling obligated to return the favor.

Play

For horses, life isn't all work and no play. Naturally curious animals, they'll approach and investigate new animals and objects: sniffing, mouthing, tasting, and even pawing at them. Foals and yearlings, in particular, spend a lot of time playing and exploring their environment. Youngsters (and some adult stallions and geldings) run and frolic together, bucking, leaping in the air, and chasing each other. They'll playfully nip, rear, mock kick, and "neck wrestle" (spar with their heads and necks).

Although horseplay may look like fun, there's no place for it in human-horse interactions. Because horses are so much bigger and stronger than us, they can hurt us unintentionally with a playful nudge or nip. Teach every horse you work with that playing with you is never okay (when he initiates it, push him away firmly and say, "No!"), then offer him another form of attention and affection—such as grooming—instead.

Horses enjoy playing with each other in many different ways, including rearing or chasing each other.

For horses who get bored in their stalls or paddocks, many companies offer "horse-safe toys like large, rubber balls." These can be a nice distraction for a young horse or a horse confined because of an injury.

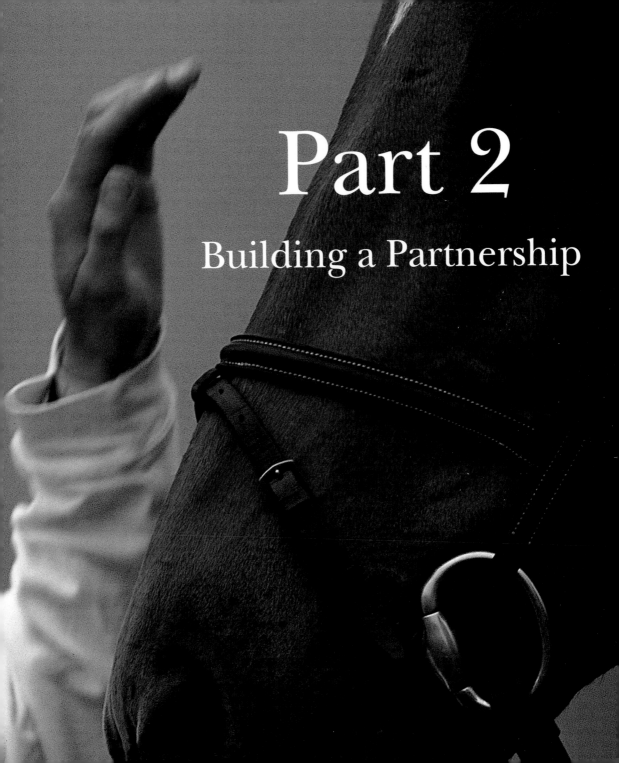

Part 2

Building a Partnership

Chapter 4

Getting Started

As you shop around for a good riding instructor, you'll notice many different styles, or "disciplines," of riding. You don't have to choose a particular discipline to focus on right away, but it will help to have an idea of what disciplines you're interested in before you select the facility where you'll begin your riding education. (Don't worry—it's never too late to change your mind. Many well-rounded horse people have backgrounds in multiple sports and disciplines.)

What Style of Riding Do You Want to Do?

The many different styles, or disciplines, of riding in the United States can be broken down into two general categories: English and western. The latter is what you see in western movies: riders in cowboy hats, boots, chaps, and spurs doing cowboy-like things—roping steers, riding the range, etc. English riders wear britches (the form-fitting pants that look like the ones football players wear) and tall, black boots or short "paddock" boots, tailored riding coats (when showing), and safety helmets.

Both styles have variations among the shapes of their saddles, but western saddles are generally bulkier, heavier (i.e., much trickier to "toss" up onto the horse), and more elaborately decorated with polished metal than English saddles. Not all riding has to be either English or western, however. For endurance competitions and trail riding, it doesn't matter what kind of saddle you're sitting in—so long as it's comfortable.

What English and western riders actually do in their saddles is very

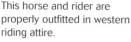

This horse and rider are properly outfitted in western riding attire.

similar at the beginning stages. You first learn to sit quietly in the saddle, maintaining your balance without pulling on the horse's mouth with the reins, bumping his back with your own backside, or swinging your legs against his sides. Then you gradually learn how to control your various body parts individually to cue the horse to do different things.

Whether you choose the English or western style of riding, the goal is to feel comfortable riding and communicating with a horse.

The goal of both English and western classical teaching methods is for the rider's cues to become so subtle that an observer notices only the horse's response—not the cues themselves. The best riders are so good at communicating with their horses that they can do it with a "whisper," rather than a "shout."

Working Together

Another goal of classical training is to help the horse

achieve his maximum physical potential in whatever endeavor you choose to tackle. By teaching a horse to carry and move his body more fluidly and efficiently, you become, in essence, his own personal trainer. The exercises and skills you practice with him help develop his muscles, cardiovascular system, and mind. Just as with human athletes, this systematic process helps to improve performance, reduce injuries, and promote overall good health.

That's not to say that your riding program has to follow a seven-days-a-week, hard-core fitness regime. Yes, the more frequently you ride, the more quickly you'll improve your riding skills. But the beauty of riding is that you can learn how to do it at any age—and at whatever pace suits your lifestyle. The majority of horse people in this country ride just for pleasure, enjoying everything from practicing their equitation skills in their backyards to taking to the trails and lining up in local parades. If you're feeling more competitive, consider one of the sports listed at the end of this chapter.

Dress the Part

Before arriving at the stable for your first lesson, be sure you have all of the necessary horsy clothes and equipment.

Safety Helmet

The most important purchase you'll ever make in your riding career is a safety helmet. Head injuries are the most common cause of fatalities in riders. A safety helmet may not be considered fashionable in every equine discipline but, if you value your brains, it should be the first thing you put on before you mount any horse. Your helmet should be ASTM/SEI-certified (American Society for Testing and Materials/Safety Equipment Institute), should fit snugly on your head, and be securely fastened at your chin. Most manufacturers recommend replacing your helmet every few years and after every fall involving a head impact.

Good safety helmets aren't cheap. So, if you're not sure how committed to riding you are, ask your instructor if she can lend you a helmet for your first few lessons. (Note: If she doesn't have an ASTM/SEI-certified helmet in your size, don't try to "make do" with a less safe helmet.)

Footwear

Whenever you're working around horses, protect your feet with sturdy boots or shoes. No flip-flops or sandals! For riding, always wear a boot with a hard sole and heel, to prevent your foot from slipping through the stirrup. If you live in a cold climate and plan to ride through the winter, insulated riding boots are well worth the extra money.

No Loose Clothing!

Matching your mount's flowing mane and tail with your own flowing clothes may sound like a pretty picture, but it's not safe. Loose clothing can catch on the saddle horn (of a western saddle), on the horse's bit, or on anything you pass by, potentially causing an accident. Some horses can be spooky about flapping clothing, such as raincoats. And your riding instructor can give you much more effective advice about your position if it's not hidden behind layers of loose clothes. Long, loose hair can even be a hazard—for example, if it gets caught on your horse's bit and he spooks suddenly. If you have long hair, just to be safe, keep it tied back in a neat braid, bun, or ponytail when you're around horses.

There's a reason why riders wear silly-looking, skin-tight britches or jeans: Shorts and loose riding pants can rub your legs raw against the saddle. Chaps and half-chaps (covering just your lower leg) are great rub-reducers, but they're illegal in the competition arenas of most English sports.

Different Sports for Different Sorts

If you're the competitive type, here are some of the more popular sports you can try with your horse. The riding styles are identified by (E) for English, (W) for western, or (B) for both.

Barrel Racing (W) – Just like it sounds, this is a sport in which riders race against time around barrels set up in a cloverleaf patter.

Breed Shows (B) – These evaluate purebreds and part-breds for the characteristic qualities that best exemplify their particular breeds. Some of the biggest shows feature breeds such as Arabians, Quarter Horses, Paints, Saddlebreds, and Morgans.

Costume Classes (B) – Offered at many horse shows, these can be a lot of fun for riders of all ages. Both you and your horse get to dress up!

Cutting (W) – This is where riders show off their horses'

This horse and rider are neatly turned out in English riding attire.

discipline and innate talent for working cattle: separating a single cow from the herd and using athletic, ballet-like moves to cut off its escape route back to the others.

Dressage (E) – A refined, ballet-like sport, dressage combines strength and precision, emphasizing subtle communication between horse and rider. Olympic-level competitors perform centuries-old skills that take years to perfect.

Endurance (B) – Veterinarians monitor the health and well-being of horses ridden in distance races, which can be as long as 100 miles or more, through beautiful countryside. Preparing your horse for this sport requires a carefully planned conditioning schedule.

Eventing (E) – This equine triathlon includes dressage,

Dressage is a centuries-old ballet-like sport.

cross-country (which tests horses' and riders' skills over ditches, banks, water, and solid obstacles), and show jumping. Each competitor must complete all three phases on one horse. An Olympic sport, eventing was originally created to test the skills, courage, and obedience of cavalry mounts.

Foxhunting (E) – Horses and riders follow hounds as they track a fox's scent. A variation known as a "drag hunt" involves chasing a fox's scent laid by a person instead of a fox.

Hunt-Seat Equitation and Show Hunters (E) – Equitation classes judge a rider's position and skills over fences (over a course of jumps) and on the flat. Show-hunter classes judge the horse's jumping style, manners, and gaits.

Polo (E) – Swinging a mallet between your horse's legs to hit a ball may sound tricky, but good polo players can do

Driving can be as challenging and exciting as riding.

Driving

Rather than riding your horse, you can sit in a cart, carriage, or sleigh hitched to him with a harness. The traditional horse and carriage has many modern-day competitive activities, including combined driving, which involves several different phases and obstacle-course-like hazards that drivers negotiate at speed. Driving is a nice option for horse enthusiasts with physical limitations.

In foxhunting, the foxhounds are led by the Huntsman as they search for a fox's scent.

it all day long. Their mounts are called polo "ponies," but most of them are actually small horses.

Polo-cross (E) – If you can't afford polo, you might want to try this fun amalgam of polo and lacrosse.

Reining (W) – This sport tests a horse's rideability and obedience, including skills such as agile spins and turns, swift acceleration, and sliding stops. This sport is considered by many to be the western equivalent of dressage because it demonstrates the horse's athleticism and responsiveness to the rider's aids.

Roping (W) – Two riders, called the header and heeler, work together to rope a cow in this example of traditional ranch work, which still is tested in today's western competitions.

Saddle Seat (E) – Riders show off their horses' fancy, high-stepping action with flair and drama in front of enthusiastic fans.

Left: Eventing is an Olympic sport that combines three phases of competition, including jumping obstacles on a cross-country course.

Show jumping is extremely popular.

Polo is a sport of kings that is now enjoyed by many around the world.

Showing In-Hand (for breed or suitability) (B) – Horse shows sponsored by different breed and sport organizations offer classes that judge a horse's conformation (structural symmetry), gaits, and temperament.

Show Jumping (E) – Horses and riders compete against the clock over colorful jump courses, aiming for clear (fault-free) rounds. This is one of the three Olympic equestrian disciplines. At non-Olympic competitions, show jumping classes often run consecutively with show-hunter and equitation classes. One of the most popular spectator sports is the puissance, or high jump.

Team Penning (W) – In one of the fastest growing sports in the U.S., riders work in teams to separate cows from a herd and gather them into a pen as fast as they can.

Tetrathlon (and Pentathlon) (E) – This sport consists of four phases: running, swimming, riding, and shooting (to make it a pentathlon, add fencing). Your performances in each phase are added up to give your final score.

Trail Classes (B) – These test riders' and horses' skills at negotiating the types of challenges they might encounter on a trail ride.

Vaulting – Like gymnastics on horses, vaulting requires strength, agility and, most importantly, excellent balance.

Racing

Galloping at top speed is one of the most thrilling activities you can experience aboard a horse. If you're not petite or brave enough to sign up for jockey silks, you can get involved as a groom, hot walker, exercise rider—or just a spectator. There are several variations of racing in this country. In addition to traditional flat racing (the kind you see in the Kentucky Derby), you may want to check out harness racing (trotting and pacing horses pulling their drivers in light, two-wheeled sulkies), steeple chasing (racing over jumps), or one of the rarer sports such as cutter racing (two-horse pairs pulling their drivers in old-fashioned chariots).

A western rider practicing the sport of cutting.

Chapter 5

Ready, Set, Ride!

If you haven't found a qualified instructor yet, now's the time. Reading books and magazines can teach you a great deal about riding, but it's safest to begin under expert supervision. (For tips on selecting a good instructor, refer to Chapter 1.) The following two chapters will explain some of the important details you should be learning in your lessons.

Tacking Up

The first few times you tack up your horse (put on the saddle and bridle), you'll probably feel a little awkward and confused, but the process will smooth out once you get the moves down. Ask an experienced horseperson to demonstrate the procedure and help you through your initial attempts. Always tie or crosstie your mount before getting started—so he doesn't wander off half-dressed. (Review the tying recommendations in Chapter 3.) If you don't have time for a thorough grooming, at least pick out his hooves and clean the areas of his body where the saddle and bridle will go. While tacking up, avoid making any sudden movements that might spook him (throwing the reins over his head, tossing the saddle up onto his back, etc.).

Saddle

Start by slowly lifting the saddle pad or blanket onto your horse's withers (the bony hump where his neck connects to his back) and sliding it back into place. The front edge should rest just behind his shoulders. If your blanket is folded, place it so the folded edge faces forward.

Before putting on the saddle, check that the girth or cinch (the belt-like strap that goes around your horse's belly, holding the saddle in place) is folded over the saddle and, if you're riding English that the stirrups are "run up." If you're riding western, also flip the right stirrup over the top of the saddle.

Holding the front of the saddle with your left hand and the cantle (back) with your right hand, approach your horse's left side. Slowly lift the saddle and rest it gently on top of the pad. Pull the pad or blanket up under the gullet (the front of the saddle) so it won't put pressure on his withers; attach the pad loops (if it has them) to the front billet on either side of the saddle. (To reach the billets, lift up the saddle flap and hold it up with one elbow.)

Next, walk under the horse's neck to the other side. If you're using an

English saddle, attach the girth to the first and third billets (if the girth has elastic on one end, attach the nonelastic end on the right side), leaving a few holes above and below the buckle in case you need to adjust it later. If you have a western saddle, drop the stirrup and cinch down, being careful not to let them swing into your horse's legs, and check that the cinch isn't twisted.

Walk back underneath the horse's neck and reach under his belly to grasp the end of the girth. Attach it to the billets on the left side and slowly tighten it. (If you have a western saddle, hook the left stirrup up over the saddle horn and fasten the cinch with either the buckle or a latigo knot—see sidebar.) The girth or cinch should be just snug enough that you can squeeze two to three fingers between it and the horse's side.

Never slide the saddle forward once it's in place. This will ruffle the hairs underneath. Instead, if you have to adjust the saddle's position, lift it and the pad up off his back, reset them on his withers, and slide them back into place.

Bridle

Before bridling your horse, unbuckle the throatlatch and—if it's an English bridle—the noseband. Some bridles may also have a curb chain and/or lip strap. Ask your instructor if these should be undone before bridling. Stand in front of your horse and slightly to his left, just far enough away so that he can't knock you in the face or chest if he moves his head suddenly.

Holding the bridle in your left hand, put one rein in each hand and slowly lift them over the horse's head. (If you're riding western, be sure the reins are tied together.) Hold the reins together beneath his neck to control him while you undo the upper, left buckle of his halter and slowly

The Latigo Knot

To fasten a cinch on a western saddle:

★ Draw the leather strap (latigo) on the left side of the saddle through the metal loop of the cinch, then bring it back up through the metal loop on the saddle. Pull the strap end to the left of the cinch.
★ Pull firmly down on the end of the strap to tighten the cinch snugly.
★ Bring the latigo from left to right just beneath the upper metal ring, then pull it back through the ring from underneath.
★ Tuck the strap through itself and pull down firmly to secure the knot.

When the saddle is in place, secure it with the girth, tightening partly while you're on the ground and again when you're on your horse.

slip it off. Loop the halter over your left elbow or hang it up. (Never throw the halter on the ground where your horse might step a foot through it.)

Now, reach your right hand under his jaw and wrap it over the bridge of his nose. Transfer the bridle from your left hand to your right, holding it in front of your horse the way it will hang on his face, with your right fingers wrapped around the top (crownpiece). Hold the bit level in the flat of your left hand and guide the bridle upward with both hands until the bit is centered in front of his lips. If he doesn't open his mouth automatically, press your thumb into the corner of his mouth (don't worry—there's a gap between his teeth here).

If your mount is "girthy" or "cinchy"—he doesn't like the girth or cinch being tightened too quickly—attach the girth loosely (but not so loosely that the saddle might slip as he moves) at first and walk him around, stopping to tighten it a few holes at a time.

As he opens his mouth, slowly raise the bridle up with your right hand and, taking care not to bump the bit into his teeth, slide it into position at the corners of his lips. (If there's a curb strap on the bridle, guide that with your left hand also, making sure it ends up under his chin, not in his mouth.)

English (left) and western (right) bridles are distinctive.

Reach up to take the crownpiece with your left hand and gently bend one ear forward at a time with your right hand while guiding the bridle over it. (If your bridle has only a small loop for one ear, put that ear through the loop and place the rest of the bridle over the other ear.) Hook a finger around his forelock (the part of his mane between his ears) to settle it in place underneath the crownpiece. Then attach the throatlatch, leaving about four fingers' widths between it and his jaw. Attach the noseband, underneath both cheekpieces, snugly enough so that you can fit one finger between it and his nose.

Finally, check that the noseband and browband are horizontal and that the bit looks even in your horse's mouth (not crinkling up his lips on one side and hanging low on the other). Tuck all of the strap ends into their respective keepers and runners (the leather loops that keep the straps in place).

The Belly Blow-up

Some clever horses and ponies learn a trick to keep the girth or cinch comfortably loose. They take a deep breath, blowing their bellies out much wider than normal, just as you try to tighten it. The girth may feel tight to you, but, when they let the air out a few moments later, it'll suddenly be loose again. That's why it's always important to double-check your girth just before mounting—so you and your saddle don't end up hanging between your horse's front legs!

The last part of securing the bridle is to fasten the noseband. Once secured, check for overall fit.

Getting On Your Horse (Mounting)

Before mounting for your first few rides, ask your instructor to check that all of your tack is adjusted properly. Then, take the reins back over your horse's head to lead him to the arena (hold both reins in your right hand, about six inches down from the bit, and carry the trailing ends with your left hand). Once in the arena, slide your stirrups down (if you're riding English), and put on your safety helmet, securing the chinstrap.

You can get on your horse either from the ground or from a mounting block. Since the latter isn't always available (for example, if you need to dismount and remount on a trail ride), it's good to learn both methods. However, mounting from the ground can pull the saddle against the side of your horse's spine, stretch the stirrup leather on that side, and sometimes even twist the saddle tree (the internal structure of the saddle). So try using a mounting block whenever possible.

The steps for mounting are the same, whether you're doing it from the ground or a block. It's good to learn to mount on either side of the horse, but get the technique down first on his left side:

★ First, check your girth, to make sure it's snug.

★ Line your horse up next to the mounting block, not so close that he bumps his leg into it, but not so far away that you'll have to take a flying leap to reach the saddle.

★ Put a rein in each hand and carefully lift them over his ears. (Don't flip the reins over his head. The quick motion can be spooky to many horses.)

★ Stand next to his left shoulder, facing his tail, with both reins gathered in your left hand, short enough so that you can control him if he tries to turn or walk off. Rest this hand on your horse's withers, just in front of the saddle.

★ With your right hand, turn the stirrup to face you and hold it steady while you reach your left toe into it.

★ Reach your right hand up to the front of the saddle and push off your right foot to bring your body up alongside your horse, turning so you're now facing the saddle. (Be careful not to poke his side with your left toe as you do this.) Then swing your right leg over his rump—being very careful not to kick him—and settle your seat lightly into the seat. With practice, you'll be able to do this step in one fluid motion.

★ Finally, place your right foot in its stirrup. If you have trouble finding it, reach down to grasp the stirrup

Check the Fit

If your horse's bridle fits properly, you should be able to:

★ See ¼ inch of the bit extending on either side of his mouth;

★ See no wrinkles in the corners of his mouth if the bit is unjointed, or about two wrinkles in the corners of his lips if the bit is jointed;

★ Fit one finger between the noseband and his cheekbone;

★ Fit one finger between his ears and the browband and crownpiece (so neither is pinching his ears); and

★ Fit at least two fingers' widths between his eyes and the sides of the bridle.

Be sure that the mounting "block" you use—which can be anything from a tree stump to a plastic stepstool—has safe, round edges that won't injure your horse if he bumps into it, and won't tip over if you lose your balance.

To get on your horse, use a mounting block whenever possible, but learn how to mount from the ground as well.

leather with your right hand and twist it so the iron faces your toe.

Unfortunately, while being mounted, some poorly trained horses fidget, step sideways, or walk away with their riders half-on. This precarious position can result in a serious accident. Ideally, the schoolhorses you learn on should know better. But, if you don't trust your mount to stand still, ask a helper to hold his bridle while you mount. Once you're in the saddle, always ask the horse to stand still for a moment while you adjust your reins, stirrups, etc. Then stroke his neck and praise him before cueing him to walk forward.

Position in the Saddle

Proper position in the saddle varies a bit depending on the sport you do. However, in all riding, the goal is to stay in balance with your horse: keeping your "center" (the area in the middle of your torso just below your belly button) directly over your feet. Imagine that, if your horse suddenly disappeared from underneath you, you'd end up standing on the ground on both feet—not falling forward onto your face or back onto your bum. When you're sitting in the saddle, an observer standing to the side should see a straight, vertical line from your shoulder to your hip to your heel. (A few disciplines, such as saddle seat, emphasize a slightly different balance in the saddle. Ask your instructor to describe the ideal position for the sport you're learning.)

Your two seatbones should be centered in the deepest part of the seat. Your upper body should be tall and straight, with your shoulders back, relaxed, and even. Hang your legs down long and relaxed, neither gripping them nor letting them flop on your horse's sides. Try to keep your "shock absorbers"—your hips, knees, and ankles—relaxed and supple, never braced. Balance the ball of your foot flat on the stirrup, neither collapsing it to the inside nor outside. And always keep your heel lower than your toes.

Your elbows should hang relaxed, close to and slightly in front of your sides. In English sports, your lower arms and reins should form a straight line from your elbow to your hand to the horse's mouth—both when viewed from the side and from above. This means that you'll have to lift your hands slightly higher when he raises his head and lower them slightly when he drops it.

In western riding, hold your reining hand just over the horn (the front) of the saddle.

Holding and Adjusting the Reins
English

English riders hold one rein in each hand, maintaining a light tension in them to maintain a feel of the bit in the horse's mouth on the other ends. (This is called "contact.") Hold your hands in relaxed fists with your wrists vertical and your thumbs on top, as if you were holding two mugs of coffee. Each rein should come from your horse's mouth, up between your ring finger and pinky finger and out the top of your fist. Hold the rein in place by gently pressing down on it with your bent thumb.

Your hands should stay between about four and six inches apart from each other. Looking down, you should see a straight line from your elbows, through your hands and reins, to the horse's mouth.

To shorten your reins, put both of them in one hand. Then slide the free hand forward to grasp the rein at the new length. Loop the pointer finger of that hand around the other rein to hold it while you slide the other hand up.

Once in the saddle, position your legs so that the ball of your foot rests flat across the stirrup and your ankle flexes comfortably.

71

Finding Your Seatbones

When you sit in the saddle, you balance your upper body on the two sled-runner-like lower branches of your pelvis. To identify exactly where these "seatbones" are, sit on the edge of an unpadded chair or stool, with both feet flat on the ground. Keeping your upper body tall and erect, slowly rock from side to side. You'll feel your weight shifting from one point of contact to another. These are your seatbones!

This rider, comfortable and relaxed in the saddle, allows her horse to walk on a loose rein.

Then check that the reins are the same length (your hands should be parallel). To lengthen your reins, simply relax your fingers slightly and let the reins slide through your hands.

Western

When riding western, your reins should be slack (looping down slightly between your hands and your horse's mouth). You can either hold the reins in two hands, like English riders, or hold both in the left, "reining" hand. In the latter case, your hand should be in the same upright-fist position described above. Hold the excess reins in your right hand, down by your thigh, about 18" away from your left hand.

To shorten or lengthen the reins, relax the fingers in your reining hand (keeping the tension in your right hand so you don't drop them) and move it up or down. Adjust the reins as necessary to make them an equal length.

Adjusting Stirrups

English

Ideal stirrup length varies from discipline to discipline and also depends on your body shape and skills. In general, the faster you're riding or the higher you're jumping, the shorter your stirrups need to be. For basic work, there are two easy rules of thumb:

★ Standing on the ground next to your saddled mount, with the stirrup iron run down to the end of the leather loop, extend your left arm in front of you, placing your fingertips on the metal stirrup bar (the part of the saddle where the stirrup is attached). Then take the iron in your right hand and pull it toward you. The bottom of the stirrup iron should just reach your left armpit.

★ Sitting in the saddle, take both feet out of the stirrups and stretch your legs down around your horse's sides. The bottoms of the stirrup irons should be about level or just below your anklebones.

Ask your instructor to show you how to adjust your stirrups safely from the saddle. Always keep one hand on the reins while you do this, just in case your horse moves suddenly.

Western

In a western saddle, check your stirrup length by standing up out of the saddle, keeping your heels lower than your toes. You should be able to fit one or two fingers between you and the seat of the saddle. It's usually easiest to shorten or lengthen your stirrups from the ground, so dismount to make any necessary adjustments. If you have a slide fastener (a square metal piece holding the stirrup leathers together), move it up closer to the saddle to shorten the stirrup or lower it to lengthen it.

Western riders often hold both reins in one hand ("reining"), freeing up their other hand to carry or do something else.

The Aids

You'll use "aids" to cue your horse while riding. The natural aids include your hands, legs, voice, and "seat."

Ideally, you should be able to use each aid independently of the others. For example, when you squeeze your right leg against your horse's side, that movement shouldn't also make you lean to the right and pull on the right rein. Independent aids are harder to develop than they sound, especially when you're trying to balance in the saddle at faster speeds.

Artificial aids include a whip and/or spurs. (When you're starting out, however, it's safest to ride without them. Don't use either without your instructor's okay.) Whips can be useful for reinforcing your leg aids, especially on lazy horses. If your horse doesn't respond to a firm kick, tap the whip just behind your leg. Occasionally, a whip can also be used to make judicious reprimands—with a quick smack on the flank or

Your "aids" include your seat, legs, hands, and voice. These are what you use to cue your horse while riding.

shoulder—however, it should never be used excessively and you should never hit a horse on his face or between the ears. If you're ever so frustrated that you're tempted to strike your horse forcefully or repeatedly, dismount immediately and call it a day.

Take care whenever transferring a whip to or accepting a whip from a person on the ground while you're in the saddle. Your horse may spook when he catches sight of the whip in the corner of his eye. Ask the person to stand close to your leg and to make the transfer slowly.

Spurs should only be worn by riders who have good balance, body control in the saddle, and coordination of the aids, as they can be very punishing on a horse. Hence the saying, "Earn your spurs."

Gas and Brakes

The first skills you'll need to learn are basic "go" and "stop" cues. To ask your horse to go faster or to move from a standstill to a walk, soften your reins (push your hands slightly forward so your horse feels less tension in his mouth), squeeze your legs gently around his sides, and either make a clucking noise with your tongue or use a voice command, such as "walk on!" Be careful not to pull your heel up when you squeeze or kick your legs; this pulls your center of gravity higher and can cause you to lose your balance. Also try to use a squeeze-and-release action, rather than gripping your horse's sides, which will either irritate him or desensitize him to your aids.

If your horse doesn't react to this aid, bump your legs gently against his sides. Finally, if you still get no reaction, kick his sides firmly with both legs. (If he's too dull to respond to this kick, ask your instructor if it'd be appropriate to carry a whip.)

To ask your horse to slow down or stop, sit still in the saddle, close your fingers around the reins, and apply a few ounces of resistance to the reins (without pulling your upper body forward or raising your hands). Hold this tension for a brief moment and then relax your arms and fingers again. At the same time, give a voice command, such as "whoa," in a low, soothing voice. If necessary, repeat the resist-and-release action in the reins, perhaps holding a little more pressure in your hands or holding for just a second longer. When he finally responds, relax the reins, stroke his neck, and praise him. Every horse is slightly different; if you're having trouble, ask your instructor for help.

Steering
English

Basic turns at the lower levels use just one rein to signal to the horse to turn in that direction. For example, if you're turning left, add an ounce or two of pressure to your left rein, without increasing the pressure in your right rein. To turn right, do the opposite.

Western

If you're holding both reins in one hand, steer your horse by "neck reining": merely move your reining hand sideways in the direction you want to go. This will bring the opposite rein against his neck, cueing him to move away from it. For example, to turn left, move your reining hand sideways several inches to the left until you feel the right rein pressing gently against his neck. Depending on his level of sensitivity, you may need to use more or less pressure against his neck to create the turn.

Dismounting

When your ride is finished, try to dismount as smoothly as you mounted. Halt your horse, put both reins in your left hand, and take both feet out of the stirrups. Pressing your hands down on his withers and the front of the saddle, lean forward and swing your right leg over his rump (again, being careful not to kick him) and drop lightly down to the ground. Slide the stirrups up the leathers (if you're riding English), take the reins slowly back over his head, and lead him back to the barn.

Untacking

To untack, simply reverse the order of the saddling and bridling process. Hang your equipment neatly out of the way as you go, so the horse can't step on any of it. Be sure to put the reins back over your horse's head and detach the throatlatch and noseband before taking off the bridle. Remove the bridle slowly, giving him time to "spit out" the bit, rather than pulling it out of his mouth, bumping it into his teeth. (This jarring, and sometimes painful experience can cause a horse to develop an aversion to wearing the bridle.) Always tie your horse up before removing his saddle.

Before putting him away, give your mount a good "rub-down." Curry or brush the area where his saddle was and rub his face with a towel, paying particular attention to the areas around his mouth and behind his ears. If his coat is sweaty and it's warm enough to bathe him, rinse him with a hose or sponge. (For more tips on grooming and bathing, review Chapter 8.)

In English riding, you steer your horse by pulling slightly on the rein that will turn your horse in the direction you want—left rein to go left, right rein to go right. Also turn your head and eyes to look ahead as this rider is doing.

Chapter 6

Basic Horsemanship

Riding is a thinking sport: In addition to coordinating and controlling two moving bodies, you have to plan where you want to go and what you want to do next, while constantly paying attention to everything else going on around you. Now and then, all of this incoming and outgoing information can overload your brain. When this happens, stop your horse, take a deep breath, clear your head, and pick just one thing to focus on. Eventually, as your muscle memory develops (your muscles learn to do their jobs without you having to consciously think about them), you'll be able to relax your mind—and enjoy the ride!

*A*gain, regular lessons with a good instructor are essential. This chapter gives you some things to think about during your lessons.

Riding the Gaits

At the walk, carry your body upright, opening and closing your elbows to allow your hands to follow the forward-and-back motion of your horse's head. Relax the muscles in your lower back and buttocks so your hips can follow the motion of his back. You'll feel your horse's belly swing from side to side, moving your legs with it: right, left, right, left, and so on. To ask him to take bigger steps, squeeze your legs alternately, thinking of using them to increase his belly's swing. For example, as his belly swings from right to left, push your right leg gently against his side.

Riding the Trot or Jog

There are three ways to ride the trot or jog, which is usually a horse's bounciest gait:

1. Posting (also known as "rising") – In the English riding style, to keep your balance in the saddle without jarring your mount's and/or your back, allow the thrust of his motion to push you a few inches up out of the saddle with every other stride. In the next stride, let your weight gently touch back down on the seat. During the "up" part of the rising trot, incline your upper body slightly forward at the hips, without hunching your back or tipping dramatically forward or backward. As you sit back down, try not to collapse at the hips and thump down into the saddle.

As you move up and down, allow your hips and knees to open and close, dropping your weight down through your ankles without letting your lower leg swing. To keep your hands steady, open your elbows as you move up and close them as you sit down. (Your horse's head and neck don't move as much in the trot as they do in the walk and canter, so, to maintain a rein contact that doesn't punish his mouth, your hands need to remain relatively still in front of the saddle.) Try not to pull yourself up

An advanced rider sitting to the trot during a dressage performance.

out of the saddle with your reins. At first, it might help to say out loud, "up, down, up, down" in rhythm with your horse's two-beat gait.

To post on the correct "diagonal," you should be rising when your horse's outside shoulder (the one closer to the fence or wall enclosing the arena, called the "rail") is moving forward—and sitting when it's moving backward. Whenever you pick up the trot or change direction, glance down briefly to be sure that you're on the correct diagonal. To change your diagonal, sit an extra beat between rising phases.

2. Sitting – To "sit the trot" in western or English riding, try to keep your seat in the deepest point of the saddle and your legs stretched down around your horse's sides. The key is to be very supple in your lower back and hips, using them to absorb most of the movement, while also trying to stay relaxed in your upper body, arms, and legs. Any tension in your body can translate into unsteady hands, which may inadvertently injure your horse's mouth—or gripping legs, which are also uncomfortable for him.

81

Practice the sitting trot for just a few strides at a time until you feel your balance and coordination improving. As you switch back and forth between rising and sitting trot, try to keep your horse's pace the same.

3. Two-point – Stand up out of the saddle so that you're balancing all of your weight on your knees (your "two points") and lower legs. Keep your heels lower than your toes (rather than pushing up off of your toes to get out of the saddle) and try to keep your calves steady against your horse's sides. Incline your upper body slightly forward at the hips, still keeping your back flat. At first, it's okay to rest your hands lightly on your horse's neck to help maintain your balance. Be careful not to use the reins to catch yourself from falling backward.

Riding the Canter

In the canter or lope, you can either use the two-point position you just read about or try to sit deep in the saddle, following your horse's three-beat motion. To do the latter well, you need to stay very relaxed and supple in your hips and lower back, allowing them to swing forward and back with each stride, while carrying your upper body tall and still. Check that your legs aren't swinging at your horse's sides. Meanwhile, as in the walk, allow your elbows to open and close with each stride, so your hands can follow the forward-and-back motion of your horse's head and neck.

Horses canter on either the right or left "lead." On a circle or turn, your mount should appear to strike off first with the foreleg on the same side as the direction he's turning. So, for example, when circling right, he should "lead" with his right foreleg. To check what lead your horse is cantering on, glance down at his inside shoulder. It should move slightly ahead of the other shoulder. Cueing

Riding in a group requires that you pay attention to the space between your horse and the other horses.

Left: This rider is in the two-point position during the canter.

Some horses kick or bite when they feel crowded. If you're mounted on this type of horse, be sure to tell other riders that he has this tendency. A red ribbon tied to a horse's tail is a universally understood sign that tells other riders, "My horse kicks. Back off!"

your horse to pick up the correct lead takes practice. Ask your instructor to help you coordinate the necessary aids.

Riding in Company

Whenever you ride with other people, maintain at least one horse's length between you and the horse in front of you and at least one horse's width between you and any horse you're passing. When passing another rider coming toward you, pass "left shoulder to left shoulder." Try to give the right-of-way to people riding faster than you or jumping courses. (If you're just walking your horse to warm up or cool down, it's usually safest to stay in the middle of the arena, so other people can work around you.)

Once you've mastered the basic skills at the walk, trot, and canter, ask your instructor if you're ready to tackle the world beyond the arena. Start with rides in large, fenced-in pastures to test your skills. Some horses are more rambunctious in the open and may try to take advantage of a tentative rider. Check that your position is secure and centered, with your heels stretched down around your horse's sides, and be prepared for the unexpected. Rather than tensing up your body—and unintentionally communicating this nervous tension to your horse—try to stay relaxed, yet alert.

Ask your instructor or another experienced rider with a calm, quiet horse to accompany you on all ventures into open spaces and trails. Just as in the arena, maintain one horse's width between your horse and hers.

Rules of the Road (and Trail)

If you're riding on public trails, learn their particular rules. On many trails, pedestrians and horses have the right-of-way over bikers. However, because you're sitting on the least predictable "vehicle," it's polite to keep a safe distance from all other trail users. Some horses spook at bicycles, rollerblades, baby strollers, etc., so avoid putting your mount in a position where he may feel trapped by a scary object. Give anything potentially spooky a wide berth and try to keep his attention on you.

Leave all gates as you found them—open or closed. Ask private landowners for permission before riding on their property and always be courteous and appreciative for this opportunity.

The Herd Instinct

Many behavioral problems arise from horses' natural instinct to stay close to the herd. For example, if you're riding a "herd-bound" horse alone in an arena, he may whinny repeatedly to his friends back at the barn. When leaving the stable on a trail ride, "barn-sour" horses may try to wheel around and run back to the barn, or may simply refuse to go forward. Horses like this are not suitable for beginners.

> Avoid riding your horse near busy roads or on narrow roads that don't have a berm or shoulder where you can ride at a safe distance from traffic. Never trot or canter on paved, rocky, or gravel roads.

One of the advantages of the equine herd instinct is a compelling desire to follow other horses. If your mount is afraid to walk past something spooky, ask a friend on an older, experienced horse to give you a "lead" (walk her horse past it). Your horse's need to "stick with the herd" will probably override his fear of the object.

After the Fall

You've probably heard the old saying, "If you fall, get right back on the horse." The underlying message—restore your confidence as soon as possible—is worthwhile but, medically speaking, it's not always the best advice. If you suffer a hard fall that knocks the wind out of you, causes pain anywhere in your body, or involves your head in any way, take a moment to catch your breath and wait for your instructor to evaluate you before you get back on. If you experienced any loss of consciousness, no matter how brief, don't remount. Concussions and spinal injuries that seem mild at first may become significant if you continue riding and don't seek medical treatment. When in doubt, consult your doctor.

Chapter 7

Training Principles

During your first few years of riding, you'll learn more from your horse than he will learn from you. However, since horses of all ages continue to learn and adapt to their situations, it's important to realize that you can change your horse's behavior, too. Whether intentional or unintentional, everything you do with him on the ground or in the saddle can either reinforce his good habits or allow the development of bad habits. Ideally, the skills you learn from your instructor and other horse people will help you do the former. Keep this in mind as you choose the experts you want to work with.

M any different training styles have emerged since horses were domesticated thousands of years ago. Unfortunately, not all of them have been fair and humane to horses. Even today, trained animal behaviorists are baffled to see some popular horse trainers using nonsensical and sometimes abusive methods. The best methods are gentle, humane and, ideally, based on the following scientifically proven principles.

Positive vs. Negative Reinforcement

The fastest and longest-lasting way to teach a horse is to use "positive reinforcement." Each time he performs a skill correctly, reward him with something positive, such as a treat or a scratch on the withers. If he doesn't perform the skill correctly, you simply do nothing at all (neither reward nor punish him). To be effective, you have to be 100 percent consistent with your cues, timing, and rewards—giving the same cue or voice command for a particular skill every time and always rewarding a correct response immediately.

The second-most effective teaching method is "negative reinforcement," more commonly known in the horse world as "pressure and release." Using this approach, a trainer applies mildly adverse pressure to the horse until the horse performs the desired skill. The trainer then immediately rewards the horse by removing the pressure. For example, to ask a horse to speed up from a walk to a trot, a rider will squeeze her legs on her horse's sides. As soon as he picks up the trot, she relaxes the leg pressure, rewarding him for doing the correct thing. Used consistently and clearly, pressure-and-release techniques can be highly effective.

Horses that have been positively reinforced for behaving in desirable ways are trusting of humans.

Animal behaviorists have proven scientifically that punishment is less effective at training horses than the two methods mentioned above. Skilled horse people can retrain even dangerous and aggressive horses more effectively with purely positive and negative reinforcement techniques. Unfortunately, many impatient and or uneducated people resort to punishing horses they're having trouble training. The results can be disastrous. A horse subjected to rough training methods may learn either to fear and distrust people or to behave even more aggressively toward them.

The line between punishment, or discipline, and abuse is often blurry in the horse world. What some might consider a firm hand or sharp reprimand others may consider inhumane treatment. The distinction is usually a matter of personal opinion. In general, though, you'll find that the best trainers elicit the greatest performances from their horses with the least amount of punishment.

One Step At a Time

Each step of the training process should logically follow the last step so the horse is never surprised or confused by a new challenge. Progress is not only faster when you break a lesson down into small steps, but the strong foundation you build makes any setbacks much easier to overcome, as well.

Whatever training method you use, plan your lessons ahead of time, breaking them down into logical steps. Always try to set your sessions up so the horse says, "Yes." Make each step so small and easy that he's sure to get it right. If he doesn't perform the skill correctly, don't reward him. If he gets confused or frustrated, go back to an earlier step that you know he can do. Then find a way to make the next step less of a challenge.

Horses can pick up new skills in just a few lessons, so be careful not to repeat and drill something too many times, which can lead to fatigue and irritability.

Giving Treats

Some trainers believe that giving horses treats can spoil them and encourage bad habits. This can happen if you're not absolutely clear about when and why you give treats. For example, if you give a horse treats every time you see him—whether or not he's behaving well—he may learn to shove his nose at you and nibble at your pockets. On the other hand, if he only receives a treat for doing something good—and if you ignore him or turn and walk away from him every time he begs inappropriately for a treat—he'll learn to behave the way you want him to, without developing any bad habits.

Some repetition is good—but too much can be counter-productive. Contrary to traditional training "wisdom," horses can pick up new skills in surprisingly few lessons. Riders who drill a skill over and over again tend to irritate and tire their horses, sometimes even causing muscle pain that makes the new skill difficult to do. The first few times you ask a horse to do a new skill, reward him for merely attempting to do it—even if he doesn't do it perfectly. Repeat the exercise once or twice more, then move on to something else. In your next session, he'll probably remember and improve his performance.

Lessons don't need to be repeated every day, either. Cross-training is as good for horses as it is for people. A horse will progress fastest, both mentally and physically, if you mix up his routine. Each time you ride, pick one or two skills to focus on. The next ride, briefly review those skills—or skip them altogether that day—and focus on something else.

Problem Solving

If your horse develops a bad habit, either on the ground or under saddle, consult your instructor immediately. She may be able to help you nip the problem in the bud before it gets too serious. If it already is serious—he's doing something dangerous like biting, kicking, bucking, or rearing—hire a professional (your instructor or other knowledgeable trainer whom you trust) to work with him. In either case, collaborate with experts to solve the problem logically and methodically.

1. First, try to determine the source of the behavior. Did something scary happen that your horse has associated with a particular activity? Is he suffering from a subtle pain or lameness? Does his saddle, bridle, or other piece of equipment fit him poorly? Are you asking

him to do more than he's currently capable of doing? Is your own behavior on the ground or in the saddle inconsistent and or confusing?

2. Treat the source of the problem: Find a better-fitting saddle, work on your cue-and-reward consistency, etc.

3. If your horse's bad behavior has become a habit, it may continue even after you've eliminated the cause. You and your trainer will need to design a series of lessons to "extinguish" the bad behavior, making his good-behavior/positive-experience association stronger than the original negative association.

4. Stay on the lookout for new sources of bad behavior. Horses have excellent memories and often make strong associations between their behavior and painful or frightening events that you may not have even considered significant. For instance, walking your horse past a flag flapping in the wind may scare him one day and cause him to swerve away from the flagpole in the future, even when the wind isn't blowing. By using positive reinforcement, you can teach him to walk quietly past the flagpole again and "un-learn" his habit of swerving around it.

Clinics: Which Ones Are Right for You?

Because horsemanship is a long-term, ongoing process, you'll progress fastest by taking regular lessons with one instructor with whom you and your horse have developed a good rapport. In addition, however, you may want to participate in occasional clinics with other trainers, either to address problems you and your instructor haven't solved or just to broaden your equine experience. To be sure that the experience is beneficial, follow these guidelines:

Charting Your Progress

Be warned: Progress isn't always linear. Sometimes a horse will have a series of positive training sessions, followed by one bad day. He may act unusually distracted or unresponsive, seeming to have forgotten all that he's learned in recent days. The good news is bad days are often followed by super days, when he performs better than he ever has before. The key is not to get frustrated during the bad ride. Accept that things aren't going well, ask the horse to perform something easy that you know he can do well, then call it a day.

If your horse has developed a bad habit, try to look at the problem from his perspective, and consult other horse owners and professionals about how to resolve it.

1. Always audit a clinic with a new trainer before taking your horse to him. Be sure you're comfortable with the trainer's methods and that they make sense to you. Watch the reactions and expressions of the horses in the clinic. Do they look relaxed and comfortable, or nervous and confused?

2. Ask about the clinician's credentials. How long has he been teaching? What are his riding/competition accomplishments? Who are his regular students and how accomplished are they?

3. During any lesson or while at any clinic, remember that, no matter how knowledgeable the teacher is or says he is, you are responsible for your horse. If you ever feel uncomfortable about how he is being treated, trust your instincts and politely tell the instructor that the treatment is unacceptable. If the trainer insists on continuing to use methods you're not comfortable with, remove your horse from the clinic immediately. It takes courage to do this, particularly in front of other participants and an audience, and especially

The Truth of the Ages

These quotes from Colonel Alois Podhajsky, Director of the Spanish Riding School in Vienna, 1939, are words to hold true even today.

"The rider with high ambitions and little knowledge will be more inclined to revert to punishment than will the most experienced rider. He will try to obtain by force what he cannot achieve by the correct use of the aids as taught by the classical school."

"To punish a horse when he has not understood a command or is unable to carry it out would shake his confidence in his rider and interfere with his progress in training. Moreover, unjust punishment or punishment which is not understood may lead to opposition. If the horse becomes aware of his strength he will measure his power against that of his rider, a situation to be avoided at all costs. On no account must a horse be punished if he is afraid, as then the fear of punishment would be added to the fear of the object that frightened him."

if the clinician is belligerent about your decision—which is highly unprofessional, but unfortunately not uncommon in the horse world—but you'll be happy later that you did what you thought was best for your horse. (This advice holds true with any other person you allow to handle your horse: farrier, veterinarian, barn help, etc.)

Clinics are excellent learning opportunities when given by qualified instructors.

Other Kinds of Training
Round-pen Training

Ground-training techniques can improve your partnership with a horse. As you work together, you'll get to know his personality better and he'll develop an invaluable trust in you, which will carry over into all of your other interactions. One of today's more popular ground-training methods, round-pen training is done in a circular pen between 45 and 60 feet in diameter, with approximately 8-foot high walls. Since there's no physical connection between you and the horse, your body language has to be even more clear and precise. The idea is to "herd" the horse in a way that mimics equine body language, thus establishing yourself as the higher-ranking animal in his mind. Your signals basically consist of

Although round-pen training has many benefits, working in close quarters with a loose horse always includes an element of risk. Ask an experienced round-pen trainer to show you how to do it safely. Whenever you're in the pen with a loose horse, keep your attention completely focused on him at all times. If you ever feel that you or he may be in danger, end the session immediately.

Some disciplines, such as dressage, prohibit the use of vocal cues and other deliberately made noises in the show ring. The skills you teach your horse with clicker training at home will carry over into his performance—just remind yourself to save the reward sound until after you leave the ring!

"go away" and "come closer" cues. By learning to herd a horse in different directions and getting him to increase and decrease his speed without ever touching him, you'll improve your own body language and teach him to pay closer attention to you.

Clicker Training

Unlike round-pen training, which uses primarily the pressure-and-release technique to teach horses, clicker training is based entirely on positive reinforcement. When used clearly and consistently, it can be a faster and longer-lasting way to teach a horse a skill on the ground or under saddle. It's also a highly effective tool for correcting problem behavior.

Have you ever seen marine mammals performing for an audience? Just as they leap into the air, you'll hear their trainer blow a whistle. That's the signal the animals have learned to mean, "You got it!" Then they swim over to a bucket of fish for their reward. This is essentially what clicker training is: The trainer gives a cue, the animal performs a skill, and then the trainer makes a distinctive sound that the animal has learned to associate with food (the reward).

The sound can be anything unique and consistent (sounding exactly the same every time you use it) that the animal can learn to associate only with good behavior. (Vocal cues, such as "good boy," are usually used too frequently in everyday activities to sound unique to a horse.) A good sound-maker for this purpose is a small hand-held "clicker," which makes a loud popping noise when you press on it.

When you first start teaching a horse with clicker training, make your rewards 100 percent consistent.

In other words, offer a treat every time you "click" a horse for performing a skill correctly. As the skill becomes a habit, gradually stop offering treats, just giving them now and then to reinforce the association of the clicking sound with something positive.

Here's an example of how you can use clicker training to teach a horse to lower his head—a skill you can take advantage of when haltering or bridling him, trimming his ears, braiding his forelock, etc., without needing to stand on your tiptoes or on a stepstool:

★ Put a halter and lead rope on your horse, and holding the lead slack, stand next to his head. Give a voice command, such as "head down," and hold a treat (a piece of carrot, apple, horse cookie, etc.) several inches below his nose.

★ As soon as he lowers his head the slightest bit, even if it's half an inch, click the clicker and let him eat the treat. (Be sure to click the clicker at the same time or immediately before he reaches the treat.)

★ Repeat this once or twice more and then end the session for the day.

★ The next time you practice this exercise, use the same voice command and hold the treat several inches lower than before. After a few sessions, keep the treat concealed in a pocket when you say, "head down." As soon as he lowers his head, click and reward.

Over a course of a week or so, you should be able to teach him to drop his nose nearly to the ground—even if he's not wearing a halter. Gradually stop giving him treats, only using them now and then to reinforce the skill

The Touch That Teaches

One innovative training technique that has gained worldwide popularity in the last several decades is the Tellington TTouch Equine Awareness Method (TTEAM). Developed by animal behaviorist Linda Tellington-Jones, this method presents solutions to common physical and behavior problems. It uses special touches, lifts, and movement exercises to release tension, increase body awareness, and identify soreness and discomfort. It also incorporates a variety of obstacles in ground exercises that teach self-control, focus, cooperation, balance, and coordination.

The goal is to encourage horses to learn without fear or force, while at the same time improving the rider's understanding and communication skills and deepening the horse-rider bond.

Biofeedback studies have found that TTEAM bodywork and exercises (such as leading a horse through a labyrinth of poles on the ground) activate all four types of brain-wave patterns in both hemispheres of the brain. One of these brain-wave patterns, beta waves, is associated with logical thinking. That's why TTEAM is known as "the touch that teaches."

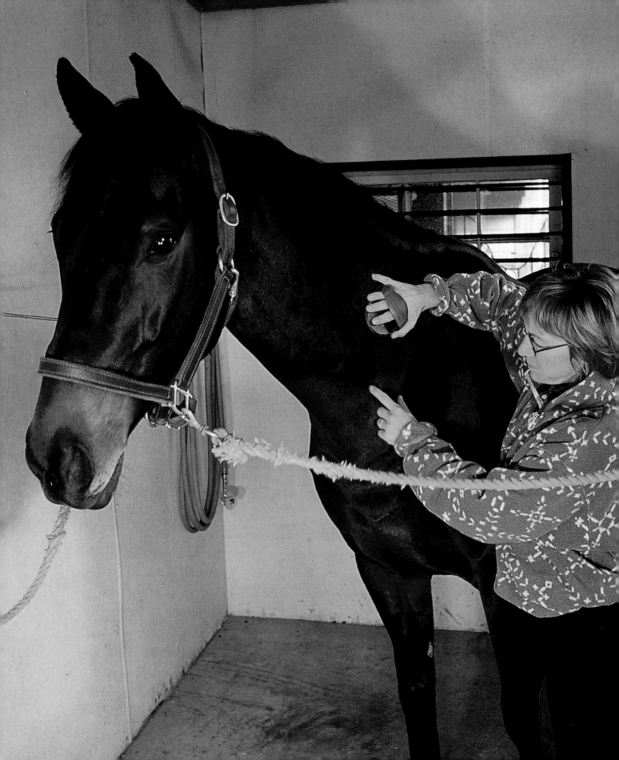

Chapter 8

Grooming

One of the best ways to bond with a horse is through grooming. As you familiarize yourself with his body and personality, he'll grow accustomed to your particular scent, voice, and movements. The more time you can spend grooming your assigned schoolhorse before a lesson, the more comfortable the two of you will be together during the ride.

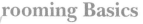

Grooming Basics

Grooming stimulates a horse's blood circulation, spreads the oils evenly through his hair, keeps his hooves clean and disease-free, and creates an overall healthy, shiny appearance. At the same time, it also gives you the chance to examine him closely for nicks, bumps, swellings, and other potential problems. Also, the cleaner your mount is, the less dirt and grime will rub off onto your tack, saddle pads, blankets, and other equipment—so grooming will save you time on tack cleaning and laundry, too.

Grooming Kit

Most teaching barns supply grooming tools for their schoolhorses. However, as you develop personal preferences for certain brushes and grooming tools, you may want to start putting together your own kit.

* *Hoof pick* – For cleaning out and removing rocks and stones from the hooves.
* *Curry comb* – For loosening hair and dirt. The best are round, firm, rubber curry combs with small teeth. The teeth wear out fast (if you're doing a good job grooming), so be prepared to replace your curry combs frequently. For extremely sensitive horses, use a softer rubber curry or rubber hand mitt. These are smaller and more flexible; their rubber "pimples" are gentler on faces, lower legs, and other sensitive areas.
* *"Dandy" or stiff brush* – For removing hair, dirt, and caked mud from the coat. (Avoid using extremely stiff brushes on especially sensitive horses. Also consider buying a stiffer dandy brush for the wintertime, when horses have thicker coats, and a softer dandy brush for the summertime, when their coats are thinner.)
* *Body or finishing brush* – Has softer bristles than a stiff brush for more sensitive areas, like the face and legs, and to give the coat a final polish.

* *Mane comb* – Heavy-duty metal or plastic combs are best. Even these can end up with broken teeth over time, so be prepared to replace them occasionally. You may also want to invest in a small, stiff brush (some people prefer "rice" brushes) to dampen and brush the mane into place.
* *Tail brush* – Different people have different preferences. One option is a human hairbrush made of soft, natural fibers (horse or boar hair), which help spread the oils in the tail without pulling out too many hairs. Look for natural-bristled brushes at your local beauty-supply store.
* *Shedding blade* – This metal blade with a serrated edge is a godsend for removing loose hair in the spring.
* *Towels ("rub rags")* – You can never have too many clean towels in the barn. They're great for finishing touches at the end of a grooming session, wiping down dusty tack, applying fly repellent, and a million other things. Any old, used towels from home will do.
* *Brush Box* – Finally, you'll need something to put all of your grooming tools in. Find a lightweight, easy-to-carry tote box (from a tack or home-supply store) big enough to fit all of your basic brushes—with a little extra room for future additions. Remember that it will be constantly bombarded with dirt and dust (that's just the nature of barns and horses), so look for one with a good cover or find an old towel to drape over it.

Grooming Tool Maintenance

There's no point in brushing a relatively clean horse with a dirty brush. Grooming tools also can harbor bacteria and fungus, which can be passed from horse to horse if you use them on more than one animal. Here are a few maintenance tips:

* To remove dirt from your brushes as you groom, periodically work the bristles back and forth against the teeth of a curry comb or the bristles of a stiffer brush. Knock the side of the curry comb against your foot or a wall. Pick long hairs out of your tail brush or comb.
* Every few weeks (or more often if you groom several horses), dunk

your grooming tools in a bucket of soapy water. Scrub each of them with a sturdy brush, then rinse the water in the bucket until it's clear. Soak the tools in a household disinfecting solution for about ten minutes. Meanwhile, rinse or wipe out your brush box and let it air dry. When the grooming tools are done soaking, rinse them again and set them in a sunny spot to dry.

★ As you clean your tools, check to see if any need replacing. Look for dull teeth on a curry comb, broken teeth in a mane comb, bent hoof picks, etc.

Grooming Precautions

Be prepared: Grooming is a messy business. Much of the dirt you clean off the horse will end up on you. So don't wear your Sunday best to the barn unless you're prepared to pay a hefty dry-cleaning bill! If you're at a horse show, wait until the very last minute to put your show clothes on, after all of the grooming is complete.

As you're grooming, remember that horses startle and move suddenly. Never kneel or sit on the ground next to a horse. Stay on your toes and keep an eye on his ears and eyes to monitor his expression, noticing when he's distracted by other things or irritated by something *you're* doing. No matter how much you trust him, never crawl under a horse's belly to get from one side to the other. And, be careful whenever walking behind him. Most horses won't kick out unless they're startled or angered. Whistle, talk, or hum to the horse while you work to let him know where you are at all times. While you're using one hand to groom him, lean into him with your other hand, not only to reassure him of your whereabouts, but also so you can sense sudden movements or tension in his body as early as possible.

Groom Regularly for Best Results

There are a lot of nutritional and grooming products on the market touted to make a horse look his best, but none of them replace good old-fashioned elbow grease. No matter how hard you try the day before a show, you won't be able to bring out a horse's best shine if you haven't groomed him regularly in the preceding weeks. Most horses enjoy being groomed (although the occasional sensitive horse may protest too-firm or too-lengthy sessions). You can even consider it part of your daily exercise routine—especially if you groom more than one horse—since doing a good job requires a certain amount of strength and endurance. There's no better way to build and tone those arm muscles!

Your daily "once-over" can take as little as 20 minutes. This chapter will walk you through the basic routine, then mention some finishing touches you'll want to add for special outings (clinics, lessons, etc.) and competitions. As you read through these instructions, refer back to the list and descriptions of necessary grooming tools in this chapter. Groom the horse in a clean, safe area (clear of tack trunks, buckets, and other obstructions), with a level floor, where you can tie or crosstie him and still have plenty of room to maneuver around him.

1. Cleaning the Hooves

Even if you don't have time for a thorough grooming, always take a minute to clean a horse's hooves and check his shoes. If he'll stand quietly for you, do this in his stall (with his halter on and lead rope attached and looped over his neck) before you lead him out of it. That way, he won't track bedding and manure down the barn aisle.

Start with a front foot: Standing next to his shoulder, facing toward his tail, gently pinch the back of his lower leg, just below the knee. He should respond by bending his knee and lifting up his foot. (If he doesn't, use a little more pressure and perhaps make a "clucking" noise with your tongue.) Wrap the hand closer to him around his lower leg to support the weight of his hoof from underneath. Then, with the hoofpick in your other hand, clean the dirt and debris out of his hoof, working in downward motions from his heel to his toe. Push the pick a little deeper into the clefts of the frog (the v-shaped structure in the middle of the hoof) to dislodge dirt and pebbles.

To pick out a hind hoof, stand alongside his leg, facing toward his tail, and slowly reach your left hand out to his hip. Slide it smoothly down his leg until you reach the tendons between his hock and ankle. Gently pinch these to ask him to pick up the foot. Support the hoof from underneath and pick out debris as described earlier.

When you finish picking each foot, slowly rest it back on the ground, rather than allowing the horse to pull it out of your hands and stamp it down on your toes.

Because grooming is a messy business, once you have your show clothes on, limit clean-up to final touches.

Never enter a stall or grooming area from which you can't exit quickly. If a horse gets nervous in a small space, he may pin you against a wall or trample on your toes unintentionally.

Flying Feet

Horses of any age may strike out or lean on you if you suddenly grab a hind leg. By putting a hand on a horse's hindquarters initially, you can avoid surprising him and, should he misbehave, use your hand as leverage to push yourself away from him.

2. Curry

Here's where you really get to use that elbow grease. With your rubber curry comb, make gentle, overlapping circles to loosen dirt, hair, mud, and dried sweat. (Think of the "wax on, wax off" motion from the movie, *The Karate Kid.*) Start with the wide, flat side of the horse's jaw, avoiding the sensitive areas around his muzzle and eyes. Then curry just behind his ears, working your way down his entire neck, chest, and shoulders. Make your way down both the insides and outsides of his front legs, finishing at the fronts of his knees. Save the lower legs (below the knees and hocks) for a gentler brush; they're usually too sensitive for the curry comb. After every few strokes, tap the edge of the curry comb on your shoe or on a fence or wall to knock off the dirt and hair collected in it.

Next, climb on a mounting block or stepstool if you need to so you can curry the withers and back thoroughly. You can lean into the horse and add a little pressure when working on any fleshier areas, particularly if he seems to be itchy in that spot (he'll tell you by sticking his upper lip out and leaning into your hands). Step back down to curry behind his elbow (an area that often gets scruffy with dandruff and dried sweat) and over his entire belly. Curry gently around his flank area, which can be a ticklish spot for many horses. Then hop on the mounting block again to work over his entire hindquarters. Finish up with the upper hind legs and the backs of the hocks, which tend to get muddy and sticky from naps on the ground.

3. Stiff Brush

By the time you've finished currying, the horse will look like a dusty, ruffled mess. So don't leave the job there! Use your "dandy" or stiff brush to remove the dirt, hair, and dandruff you loosened with the curry comb. Again, start at the head and work your way down and back over his body.

Gently brush his face in the direction of the hair growth, sweeping the loose hairs and dirt off of his head. Hold his forelock (the "bangs" of his mane that fall over his forehead) to the side and either brush it out with the stiff brush or comb through it with your mane comb. Brush or comb the rest of his mane, too. Then move on to his neck, using short, flicking motions of the stiff brush in the direction of his hair growth. Continue this down his shoulder and legs—brushing more gently over the sensitive lower legs— all the way to the bulbs of his heels.

Work your way back over the entire body (using the stepstool again to reach his withers, spine, and rump). Pay attention to easy-to-miss places: under the mane, behind the elbows, underneath the belly, between the hind legs, etc. The hair whorls over the flank area may be a little tricky to brush until you get the hang of it. Brush up the middle first, in the direction of the hair. Turn your brush, following the fan-like hairs out to one side, then follow the hairs in the reverse direction on the other side. Finish off by thoroughly brushing the hindquarters and down the hind legs.

4. Final Polish

At this point, the horse should appear fairly respectable. If you have a little more time or you want him to look especially spiffy for a lesson or clinic, carry on with the final polish.

Using longer, sweeping strokes, polish his entire coat with the soft body brush, still working in the direction of the hair growth. Just as with the stiff brush, frequently rub the brush's bristles against the teeth of your curry comb to remove hair and dirt.

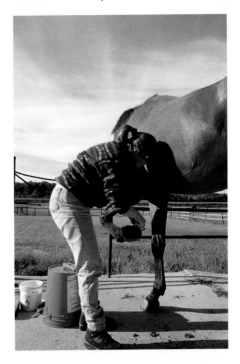

When you clean a horse's hoof, support it underneath with one hand and use the other to hold your hoofpick, scraping out dirt and debris.

Dampen your stiff brush, mane comb, or mane brush (a small, stiff-bristled brush) and lightly brush the mane, starting at the roots of the hairs. This will help it lie flat on the neck.

Finally, use a rub rag to wipe off any remaining dust on his coat. Then dampen a clean sponge and gently wipe the area around his eyes to get rid of any "eye boogers." Rinse the sponge thoroughly and wipe his nostrils and muzzle clean.

Save the Tail!

Everyone loves to see a horse with a thick, full tail. Unfortunately, maintaining such a tail isn't easy. Every time you brush out a tangle, you pull out precious tail hairs—and *all* tails get tangled. No matter how much care you take, a horse might feel an itch one day and rub his tail on the fence, breaking delicate hairs—or his buddy might decide to bite a chunk out of it. So, do the best you can, then keep your fingers crossed! Here are some tips:

⋆ Shampoo (rinsing very thoroughly) and condition the tail whenever it appears stained or dirty—even as often as once a week.

⋆ Spray the tail with a specially made shining or detangling product or try dipping it in a mixture of vinegar and hot water (about one cup of vinegar per two gallons of water) after washing it. On days when you don't need to shampoo the tail, but would like to brush it out, first spray it with a little detangler to minimize tangles. (If you plan to braid the tail for a show, don't spray this on the top half of the tail because it'll make the hair too slippery to work with.)

⋆ Allow the tail to dry thoroughly before brushing or combing.

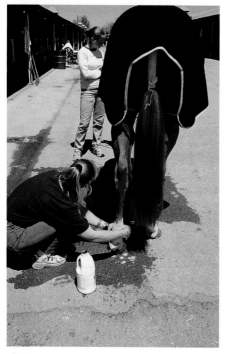

This horse's tail has been bandaged to smooth down the hairs and his white feet are getting extra attention so he'll look his best when he's being shown.

⋆ Take your time brushing out the tail, section by section. Separate each small section away from the rest and, using a clean, soft brush, comb, or just your fingers, starting at the very bottom of the hairs, stroke slowly through them and work your way up to the tailbone. When you reach a tangle, tease it apart slowly so as not to tear out any hairs. When you finish, you should be able to run your fingers through the entire tail without snagging them on a knot.

Post-Exercise Rinse/Rub-Down

After a sweaty workout, if the weather's warm, rinse your mount off with plenty of water, especially in the areas that were under his saddle, bridle, and other tack. Dried sweat can irritate the skin and contribute to hair loss and fungal infections. Either spray him down with a hose or fill a bucket with clean, lukewarm water (if possible), and use a soaked sponge to rinse these areas until no more sweat bubbles run off his body. Then gently scrape off the water with a sweat scraper, moving in the direction of his hair growth. Be careful using the sweat scraper over bonier areas, like the withers and hips, and don't use it on the lower legs. Instead, run your hand down the fronts and backs of the legs to squeeze out excess water. Empty and thoroughly rinse the bucket and sponge after use.

Frequent washing can over-dry a horse's coat and hooves, particularly if you use shampoos and soaps. So, try to limit your shampooing to pre-show baths or spot-washing (just shampooing areas that are stained or especially dirty). To protect the hooves, apply a hoof moisturizer before washing. Afterward, use a towel to rub the legs dry, so water doesn't continue dripping down on the hooves.

The Mud Factor

Some horses love to roll in mud. On a really wet day, a horse may come in from the pasture an entirely different color. The best way to cope with this, if you have the time, is to wait until the mud dries, then brush it off with a stiff brush. Use a curry comb to loosen any really tough patches. If you don't have time to wait for the mud to dry and if it's warm enough to bathe him, wash the mud off with a spray nozzle, go over him with a sweat scraper, and rub him dry with towels.

Giving Your Horse a Bath

It helps to have someone with you when you give your horse a bath. Unless they're very used to it, horses tend to move around while being bathed. Your helper can hold your horse so you can better focus on the job.

Before you get started, make sure you have all the supplies you'll need on hand: a long hose attached to a spigot with hot and cold running water so the water comes out warm, or several buckets of

If it's too cold to wash the horse, rub his sweaty areas as dry as you can with a clean towel. After he's dried completely, curry these places again to loosen the dried sweat and dirt, then brush them clean.

lukewarm water for rinsing. You'll need shampoo, a large sponge, curry comb or grooming mitt, sweat scraper, mane comb, and a couple of clean, dry towels.

When you do bathe a horse with shampoo, dilute it in a bucket of water, blasting it with the hose to create lots of suds. Thoroughly soak his coat with the hose or clean, warm water before sponging the sudsy water onto him. Work in sections, just as you do grooming, starting at the head and making your way down the body. Be very careful not to get water or soap in his eyes and ears. Getting water in the ears is a particularly uncomfortable experience for horses, sure to turn them off of bathing for a long time.

As you apply the soapy water, work it into the coat

Don't forget to rinse hard-to-reach areas like the stomach and between the legs.

with a curry comb or rubber grooming mitt. Spend extra time scrubbing white spots and markings. Then rinse thoroughly with water and, if the water is still running off dirty, repeat the process.

When your horse is thoroughly rinsed, go over his body with the sweat scraper to get as much water off as possible. Then rub him down with a clean towel or two.

To add a little polish to your horse's coat and make stains easier to remove later, spray him lightly with a coat conditioner or polish after bathing while he's still damp. Rub it into his coat with your hand or a brush, then allow it to dry. (These products make the coat shiny and *slippery*. So, be careful not to spray them on the saddle area, the mane or top of the tail—if you plan to braid them—or the lower legs—if the horse will wear protective boots or bandages before his next bath.)

Shampoo, Conditioner, and Other Products

Just about any equine or human shampoo and conditioner on the market will work on a horse's coat, mane, and tail. Avoid detergents, such as dishwashing and laundry soaps, which strip the natural oils from the hairs. For gray and white horses, buy the purple shampoos (or "bluing") made specifically for gray hair. Use this to scrub white legs clean, too. Many other products, ranging from coat polishes to tail detanglers, may give your grooming job that extra "edge," but nothing will replace good, old-fashioned elbow grease!

Trimming Tips
Shortening and Thinning the Mane

The preferred look in some breeds and disciplines is a long, natural-flowing mane. In others, it's thinner and

Getting Help to Clip

If you decide to body clip your horse, ask a knowledgeable horse person to show you how to do it. When you're finished, be sure to cover the missing coat sections with blankets to protect your horse from the cold and wind, particularly when he's outside. He'll be especially vulnerable just after he's been clipped, when the hair is shortest. As the hair grows back in, you may be able to back off on the blanketing (use lighter blankets or just blanket during the coldest times of the day).

Vacuuming

One of the best ways to cut down your grooming time is with a vacuum—one made specifically for horses. A vacuum can be great for removing dried mud and ground-in dirt. The noise of the machine and sucking feeling on his skin will be alarming at first, so introduce it to a horse very slowly. Once he's comfortable with the sound, rub the nozzle gently over his shoulder and neck. Stay clear of bony and ticklish areas. Keep the vacuum located far enough away from the horse so he can't kick or bump into it. If you have to move it, try not to startle him with quick motions or loud noises. Most importantly, keep the power cord safely away from his teeth and hooves.

shorter. In sports such as dressage and show hunters, multiple small, neat, evenly-spaced braids are the norm. These are easiest to make when the mane is about 4 to 5 inches long and an even thickness throughout.

To shorten and thin the mane, most people pull it out a few hairs at a time. As you can imagine, this isn't a comfortable experience for horses. To make it less painful, pull a horse's mane on a warm day after he's exercised—when his skin is soft and his pores are open. Don't try to pull the entire mane in one session. Do a little bit at a time over several days or weeks. Then, rather than letting the mane grow very long again, touch it up now and then with brief pulling sessions. That way, you'll never be tempted to rush the process and pull more hairs at a time than he can tolerate.

Here's how to do it: Stand next to him on a mounting block, so your eye level is even with the ends of his mane. Use a short-toothed mane comb to remove any tangles. Then, a small section at a time, grasp a few of the longest hairs with your fingertips and "tease" the rest of the section by combing the hairs up toward their roots. Pull the long hairs out with a swift, firm yank. (If the horse flinches, you pulled too large a chunk of mane. Try to pull less hairs the next time.) Comb the mane down again and go on to the next section. Every now and then, step back to see where the mane looks uneven, then pull the longer sections to tidy them up.

For horses who really protest having their manes pulled (and some do), try using a tool designed to thin and shorten manes, such as a Grooma® Mane Master®. These devices are a great pain-free alternative to mane pulling, although they create thicker chunks of hair closer to the roots, which make braiding difficult.

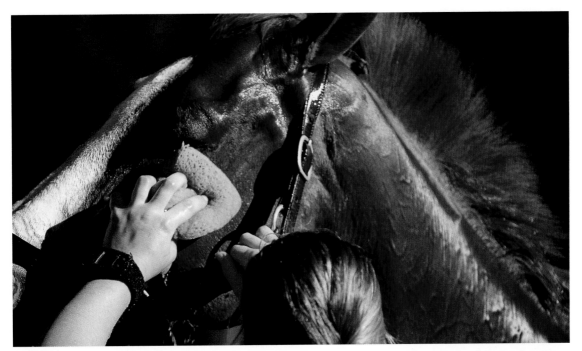

Tidying the Face and Legs

In some breeds and disciplines, horses get fairly elaborate "hair cuts" to enhance their best qualities in the show ring. For the average horseperson's purposes, however, the only hair trims you might want to do are his bridle path and fetlocks.

The bridle path is the little area of mane underneath the bridle's crownpiece (the strap that goes behind the horse's ears), which can get tangled and sweaty over time. To keep things neat and clean, clip one to two inches of mane down to the roots, starting just behind the line between the horse's ears and working your way backward down the neck. You can either do this with blunt scissors or clippers (available through tack stores and catalogs). If you use the latter, spend plenty of time getting your horse accustomed to the noise and vibration before trying to clip any hair. Play gently with his ears now and then, too, so he gets used to being touched in that ticklish area. (Never use electric clippers or any other electric devices in a wet wash stall.)

Horses have sensitive faces, and it's best to clean and rinse them using a damp sponge and working gently around the eyes, ears, and nose.

To give a horse's legs a more refined appearance, clip the long hairs growing from the point of the fetlock (the ankle joint). Trim them to a length even with the surrounding hairs, using blunt scissors or clippers. (Not all horses grow long fetlock hairs, so this may not be necessary with every horse.)

Tail Tricks

Different tail styles are popular in different breeds and disciplines. In the hunter ring, for instance, the tail should grow to a long, natural point at the end and the top hairs should either be left long or braided in a neat, French braid. Dressage and event horses often sport "banged" tails—cut horizontally at the bottom just above the fetlocks (for dressage) or about halfway between the hocks and fetlocks (for eventing). The tops of their tails are shaved on the sides to create an hourglass shape.

Ask an expert in your particular discipline to show you how to trim your horse's tail appropriately for the show ring.

Braid Like a Pro

In many disciplines, horses' manes—and sometimes tails, too—are expected to be braided. Good braiding "jobs" are much more difficult than you might think. Not only do the braids have to be neat, even, and flattering, they have to *stay* that way throughout the competition. Find out what traditional length, size, and number of braids is appropriate for your horse's breed or discipline. Then ask an expert braider to demonstrate his or her technique. After that, it's just a matter of practice, practice, practice!

Braids are either secured with rubber bands or yarn. In most disciplines, it's best to use the color that most closely matches your horse's mane and tail color. If you use yarn, select a strong brand that won't break easily. Be very careful removing yarn braids after the show. (A seam-ripper, available at sewing stores, is a great tool for this purpose.) Try not to cut any chunks of mane out as you cut the yarn. If you do, your next braiding job will be much trickier! One last word of advice: If you can't braid well, don't do it at all—or pay an expert to do it. A tidy, well-brushed mane is much more attractive than a collection of loose, sloppy braids sticking out in all directions.

Body Clipping

As the days shorten, horses grow long, fuzzy winter coats, which are great for keeping them warm, but sometimes not so efficient for riding. If you exercise a furry horse hard in an indoor arena, he'll probably work up a heavy sweat. Because his hair is so long, it may take *hours* for him to dry out. This makes him vulnerable to catching a chill.

To prevent this from happening—and to cut down on grooming and rubdown time—many people "body clip" their horses. Using heavy-duty electric clippers, they shave either the entire coat or the areas most likely to get sweaty during a workout (chest, neck, etc.). Even a very minimal two-inch horizontal clip down each side of a horse's body can help him release heat while working and cool down faster after a workout.

A braided mane is required for showing and other competitive or formal events. Ask a pro to show you how to do it if you want to learn. Braids are secured with small rubber bands or yarn.

Part 3

Selecting Your First Horse

Chapter 9

Deciding What You Want

When you and your instructor decide you're ready to own or lease your first horse, ask her to guide you through the selection process. This is the most important time to have professional help. In exchange for this service, she may charge you an hourly rate or 10 to 15 percent of the horse's purchase price, but it'll be well worth it. Your first horse will be the most important teacher in your riding education, so it's very important to find just the right one.

*B*y now, you should have an idea of what discipline or disciplines you're interested in. This will help you and your instructor narrow down the search. Although some horses excel in one or two particular disciplines, most "first horses" (horses suitable for beginners) are versatile enough to do a variety of jobs. Certain breeds and types of horses might be better at some disciplines than others. But, with so much variety within each breed, it wouldn't be fair to say that a horse of a certain breed couldn't succeed at a particular sport. The important thing to remember is that every horse is an individual and should be judged on his own merits, as well as on general factors such as breed, age, and sex.

Pretty Is as Pretty Does

It's easy to fall for a pretty horse with an adorable face, and ignore the old saying, "You don't ride the head." Looks matter somewhat—after all, this is the face that will greet you every day over the stall door—but your decision to buy should be based on more practical criteria: temperament, age, ability, and soundness. Of these, temperament should be Number One.

Horses have as many different types of temperaments as people do. Some are hot-tempered and moody. Others are mellow and lazy. Some will work all day for you, with seemingly endless energy. The real gems, especially for beginner riders, are the ones who will tolerate your mistakes and continue to perform for you day after day without complaint.

Since you'll probably spend more time grooming and caring for your horse than actually riding him, his behavior on the ground must be agreeable. Not all horses learn proper "barn manners" growing up. Instead, some learn to bite, kick, and/or run over people. Horses who were cooped up in stalls too much as youngsters sometimes develop destructive habits such as weaving (walking back and forth in the stall) and cribbing (biting at parts of the stall or fence and gulping in air, making a strange burp-like noise). Generally, it's best to avoid buying a horse with poor ground manners or bad habits.

Age vs. Experience

Depending on the discipline, most horses' careers peak somewhere between ages 7 and 12. Their value, consequently, is usually highest during this time, too. Horses who are either younger or older than this range are generally more affordable. An exception to this rule is racing, from which most horses retire before they're even full-grown—often due to injury.

The description "older and wiser" is just as apt in horses as in people. Older horses tend to have more training and experience under their belts (girths). They're usually more reliable and better at adapting to new situations, because they've "been there, done that." Young horses, on the other hand, are much better off in the hands of professionals, who can channel their youthful energy into productive training. When ridden by inexperienced riders, young horses often develop bad habits and become "sour" (resentful and uncooperative) about their work. Now and then, with the help of a professional trainer, a generous young horse and a novice rider with excellent instincts become a successful pair. In general, however, the early training of young horses is best left to the experts.

An older, dependable horse is usually the better choice for novice riders.

The "Learning Together" Mistake

When you go to school, you expect your teacher to know more than you, right? Well, the same is true in riding, only the teacher in this case is your horse. The more experienced your horse is, the faster and happier your learning experience will be. The opposite is true, too: When beginner riders make the mistake of buying inexperienced ("green") horses, it's like the blind leading the blind. So wait until you've developed your own skills on a "schoolmaster" before riding a green horse.

He Says, She Says

Another group of horses best left in the hands of experts is stallions—particularly active-breeding stallions. Many of these strong, handsome guys have wonderful temperaments, but their overabundance of hormones tends to make them more difficult to handle, especially around mares in season. Geldings don't have these hormones to deal with; their less virile behavior makes them simpler and safer to handle.

Mares experience heat (estrus) cycles through the spring and summer. For many mares, these cycles have little or no effect on their personalities and performance. Some mares, however, seem to become more irritable and possibly even physically uncomfortable when they're in heat. Veterinarians can prescribe an effective, yet costly, hormone treatment to reduce these symptoms.

Some people prefer working with one gender more than another. However, mares, geldings, and stallions have all reached the top ranks of the sporthorse world. In most sports (excluding racing, where colts and geldings are generally faster than fillies), there doesn't seem to be a significant difference in their strength or athletic ability. Again, it's more important to evaluate each horse as an individual.

Talent to Do the Job

Just as we can't all slamdunk like Michael Jordan, not every horse can race like Secretariat or jump like Olympic silver-medalist Gem Twist. Many first-time horse buyers hunt for the Secretariats and Gem Twists but, oftentimes, such talented animals are "too much horse" for beginners. Talent and temperament don't always go hand in hand. This is why it's so important to rely on your instructor's judgment and experience while selecting your first horse. You need a safe, reliable partner to show you the ropes. Save the Secretariats and Gem Twists for later in your riding career.

Nobody's Perfect

One of the most popular pastimes of horse people is to critique horses' conformation—the structural symmetry and shape of their bodies. "Form is function," people will tell you. In other words, good conformation may contribute to a horse's athletic abilities—and poor conformation may predispose him to unsoundness (lameness). Although no golden rule for perfect conformation exists, most horse people agree on certain ideal qualities (straight legs, well-proportioned bodies, etc.). Very few horses are so well put together that an expert would call them conformationally perfect.

Rely on your instructor to decide whether or not a horse's conformation will interfere with the job you want him to do. Here are some basic faults she'll be looking for:

★ *Small feet* – Horses with feet that are small in proportion to their bodies can be prone to chronic foot pain.

★ *Short, straight pasterns* – If you're planning on doing any demanding work, such as jumping, avoid a horse with extremely short, straight pasterns, which seem to predispose horses to arthritis in the pastern joints.

★ *Extremely "turned-out" or "turned-in" front legs* – Not only does such conformation increase the risk of a horse hitting and injuring one leg with the other, it also causes an imbalance in the forces impacting the leg when it touches the ground. This can contribute to pain and unsoundness in the feet or legs.

Soundness

One of the most crucial qualities to evaluate in a new horse is soundness (freedom from lameness, stiffness, or other obvious physical discomfort). For all of their power and strength, horses can be rather fragile. A wide

variety of problems, ranging from back soreness to hoof and tendon injuries, can put a horse out of commission for days, weeks, or even months. These problems result in costly veterinary bills and countless hours of time spent nursing your horse back to health—not to mention the pain and suffering endured by the patient himself.

Some injuries and ailments are unavoidable, no matter how hard you try to protect your horse. But, as you'll read later in this book, there are *many* things you can do to make his surroundings safer and keep him in the best health and condition possible.

Conformation can play a role in his susceptibility to soundness problems but, even more importantly, a horse's soundness history (which an honest seller should share with you) can be a great predictor of his future durability. During the prepurchase exam (discussed in Chapter 12), your veterinarian will be able to perform a range of tests to evaluate the horse's current soundness, to identify scars and other irregularities that may indicate past problems, and to evaluate his capacity to stay sound performing the job you want him to do.

Many suitable "first horses" have accumulated a certain amount of wear-and-tear (arthritic joints, for example) over the years. Some of these problems can be maintained with good veterinary and shoeing care. Before you start shopping for a horse, discuss with your instructor, veterinarian, and farrier (horseshoer) what soundness issues you'll be willing to live with.

Want Wheels?

Not all horse sports involve sitting in a saddle. Many horses can be trained to pull a wheeled cart, carriage, "buggy," or sleigh (if you're traveling on snow) behind them—just like the horses who provided transportation for people back before cars were invented. Taking up the reins of a "driving" or "harness" horse can be as challenging and exhilarating as riding. (A driving horse is hitched to the vehicle via a network of leather straps, called his "harness.") Starting out, you'll want to get plenty of expert instruction and advice. If you're interested in buying a driving horse, look for the same desirable qualities as in a riding horse: good temperament, experience, soundness, etc.— and find a knowledgeable driver to help you shop.

Left: Because injuries can sideline a horse for long periods of time, it pays to give his legs plenty of care and attention.

Chapter 10

Popular Horse Breeds

W

With hundreds of horse breeds

in the world, you're sure to find one

just right for you.

This chapter tells you about just a

few of the popular breeds

in the United States

(and the world) today.

American Quarter Horse

When you picture the classic cowboy riding the range in the American West, the horse you're imagining him on is most likely an American Quarter Horse. This compact, heavily muscled animal is the quintessential cow horse. Still earning his keep on many cattle ranches across the country, the American Quarter Horse also dominates western sports, from cutting, reining, and roping to western pleasure and trail classes. American Quarter Horses and American Quarter Horse-Thoroughbred crosses, known as "appendix American Quarter Horses," are successful in many English disciplines, too.

On the racetrack, the American Quarter Horse is the world's fastest equine sprinter. He can race a short distance faster than any other horse: a quarter mile in 21 seconds or less!

The Arabian has a distinct and honorable heritage.

Arabian

The beautiful, graceful, intelligent Arabian is believed to be the world's oldest-known breed of riding horse. Originally bred in the deserts of the Middle East thousands of years ago, this horse is known for his stamina and soundness. Most modern horse breeds in the United States descend from this ancient breed.

The Arabian's most distinctive characteristic is his chiseled head with a dished profile, broad forehead, curved ears, and large, wide-set eyes. His neck is long and elegant and his body is light-framed and refined. Although he has a vibrant, energetic personality, his trainability and gentle disposition make him a wonderful mount for all ages. Arabians excel in endurance sports, but they also perform well in western and English sports, such as cutting, reining, jumping, and dressage.

The Baroque Influence

Like the Arabian, ancient breeds from the Iberian Peninsula, known as "Baroque" breeds, have profoundly influenced many other breeds. The **Spanish Andalusian** and his cousin, the **Portuguese Lusitano**, are believed to have been ridden as early as 4,000 B.C.E. Prized as war horses in earlier times, they evolved into bullfighting mounts and then eventually into classical dressage horses. Their strength, impulsion, and natural collection, coupled with a kind temperament, make them excellent riding horses.

Among the European warmblood breeds that can trace their roots back to the Andalusians and Lusitanos are the dramatic **Friesians** (known for their high-stepping action and talent for driving and dressage) and legendary **Lipizzans**.

Most people think of Quarter Horses as quintessential western horses, but their versatility makes them excellent mounts for all kinds of riding.

The Baroque influence is also evident in U.S. breeds, including the American Quarter Horse, Appaloosa, Paint, and mustang.

The stars of the Walt Disney movie, *Miracle of the White Stallions*, Lipizzan stallions are the exclusive mounts of classical dressage masters at the Spanish Riding School in Vienna, Austria. Their spellbinding performances include the dramatic "airs above the ground": rearing and leaping into the air with incredibly controlled power.

Horses (and Ponies) of Color

European explorers and Native Americans deserve the credit for developing several unique, colorful horse breeds. The first spotted horses introduced to the Americas are believed to have crossed the ocean with the Spaniards. The finer-boned European blood mixed with the sturdier wild horse populations, which were then domesticated by Native Americans.

In the Northwest, the Nez Perce tribe hunted buffalo from the backs of strong, intelligent, spotted horses now called **Appaloosas**. Today, the easy-going Appaloosa makes a wonderful family horse. A smaller version of the Appaloosa, the Pony of the Americas, models similar spotted coat patterns.

Appaloosas, with their tell-tale spotted patterns, were the horses ridden by the Nez Perce Indians.

Horses with larger spots were the mounts of the Comanche Indians. These were the ancestors of today's **Pinto** and **Paint** horses, who are now popular in both English and western sports.

Draft Horses

The heavyweights of the horse world are the drafts. These big-boned, powerful animals were originally bred as war and work horses. Today, you can still see some draft horses at work in the field or in pulling contests at shows and fairs. Most Americans will recognize the Budweiser Clydesdales who pull the Anheuser-Busch beer wagon. Drafts and draft crosses also make good pleasure horses, dressage horses, and even jumpers. Usually gentle, willing animals, full drafts can weigh as much as 2,600 pounds.

Equine Mutts?

When you buy a horse, ask the seller if he has "papers." These prove that he's registered as a purebred or half-bred with his respective breed organization. (They also prove that the seller legitimately owns the horse.) You'll need them if you plan to compete in breed-specific shows. There's no shame in having a horse with no papers, though. Some of the best international sport horses have been "mutts"—or crossbreds—of mixed heritage.

You can see how big-boned this Clydesdale foal is. He will grow into a strong work horse.

Gaited Horses

Several horse breeds in this country evolved to suit the topography of the rolling farmland and plantations of the South. The **Tennessee Walking Horse**, **Missouri Fox Trotter**, **American Saddlebred**, and other "gaited" breeds can coordinate their legs in ways that don't fit the normal footfall patterns of the gaits described in Chapter 1. The slow gait, rack, running walk, foxtrot, single-foot, and pace are all slightly different variations of "easy-riding gaits." These ultra-smooth gaits are so steady that riders describe the experience as "sitting on butter" or "riding on air." Historically, plantation owners could spend hours on the backs of these horses, traversing their properties and overseeing their crop workers.

Today, gaited horses are most popular in the show ring and on the trail. The "peacock of the horse world," the American Saddlebred moves with a dramatic high-knee action, carrying his head high, and eyes and ears sharply focused. Despite his excited appearance in the show ring,

An elegant Saddlebred, known as the "peacock of the horse world."

the American Saddlebred is known for his unflappable good sense and people-oriented personality.

The spirited and refined **Paso Fino**, a gaited horse selectively bred in Latin American countries for centuries, is also rapidly gaining popularity in this country.

Miniature Horses

Technically, all mature horses 14.2 hands or smaller are considered ponies—but these tiny equines are the exception to the rule. They're Miniature Horses! Full-grown, they're no bigger than large dogs, weighing between 150 and 250 pounds. Centuries of careful breeding have created these elegant, scaled-down versions of the normal-size horse. Although only children smaller than 70 pounds are suitable mounts for them, Miniature Horses can participate in many different sports, including driving, jumping (unmounted), costume classes, and obstacle courses. They can live on as little as one-third of an acre and their maintenance costs are one-tenth of those of full-size horses.

Driving is a popular sport for Miniature Horses.

The Morgan is a stylish yet versatile breed.

Morgan

Unlike most horse breeds, which are bred for particular sports, the Morgan Horse is bred specifically for his versatility. A small, compact horse with a muscular body, the Morgan is known for his soundness, power, agility, and stamina. His stylish movement makes him a talented driving horse, but he also excels under saddle in dressage, saddle seat, cutting, reining, jumping, endurance, and more. His gentle personality and comfortable gaits make him a valuable therapeutic riding horse, as well.

Pony Power

After centuries of surviving severe climates and rugged terrain in the wild, most pony breeds have evolved to be especially short, sturdy, sound, and intelligent. For years, ponies were popular work animals in coal mines because of their ability to travel into narrow mine shafts. Their strength and endurance also suited them to farmwork—pulling plows or packing heavy loads on their backs.

Today, ponies are most commonly used as mounts for children and small adults. They're also seen pulling wheeled carriages in sports such as combined driving, where they can be driven by people of all ages and sizes. Extremely versatile and athletic, ponies are capable of competing in most equine sports. In dressage, for example, they are rapidly replacing larger horses as suitable mounts for small riders.

The **Shetland**, one of the smaller pony breeds, is a popular first mount for kids. **Welsh** and **Connemara** ponies are treasured for their excellent jumping talent. The high-stepping **Hackney** pony, on the other hand, is most commonly seen in harness in driving competitions. Many other pony breeds, such as **Dartmoors** and Australian, British, and German **Riding Ponies**, are gaining influence in America.

Ponies are popular mounts for children—but don't let their small size fool you. They are strong and smart.

Crossbred ponies, which may include blood from two or more different breeds (including horse breeds), are also popular children's and small adults' mounts. The Welsh/Thoroughbred cross, for example, is highly successful in the show-hunter pony ring. Occasionally, some full-blooded horses, such as Arabians, Morgans, Appaloosas, American Quarter Horses, and even Thoroughbreds, simply don't grow taller than the 14.2-hand mark so, technically, they're considered ponies, too.

Standardbred

Pulling their drivers in lightweight vehicles, called sulkies, inches behind their flying hind hooves, Standardbreds race at speeds of 30 miles per hour or faster. These "harness racers" resemble Thoroughbreds, but have slightly shorter, longer bodies and bigger, sometimes "Roman-nosed" heads.

On the "harness track," Standardbreds compete in either trotting or pacing races. Whereas trotters travel in the traditional

One rule of thumb to remember: Never underestimate a pony. Although small in stature, ponies have a disproportionate amount of strength, talent, and personality! They're often more clever—and more mischievous—than horses. A rider who "earns her spurs" on a difficult pony will easily master her first horse.

diagonal gait (left front and right rear legs moving in unison, and right front and left rear legs moving in unison, with all four legs suspended in the air between each stride), pacers move the legs on one side of their bodies in tandem (right front and right rear moving in unison, left front and left rear moving in unison, with a moment of suspension between each stride). Known for their docile, willing temperaments, off-the-track Standardbreds find second careers in a variety of disciplines, from barrel racing to dressage, saddle seat to combined driving.

Thoroughbred

One of the best-known descendents of the Arabian is the Thoroughbred. Slightly larger and heavier than his cousin, the Thoroughbred is bred primarily to race. (However, a small percentage of Thoroughbreds and Thoroughbred crosses in this country are bred specifically for non-racing sports, such as jumping and eventing.) Thanks to centuries of careful selection, this equine running machine can race at speeds greater than 40 miles per hour.

Thoroughbreds are best known as racehorses, but they excel at many sports, including steeplechase racing.

Because the careers of most racehorses are over by age five or six, young Thoroughbreds are often retrained to compete in other disciplines. Many top jumpers, hunters, steeplechasers, and eventers are ex-racehorses. Some "off-the-track" Thoroughbreds even find themselves playing polo, patrolling city streets in mounted-police units, and acting in movies.

Warmbloods

For the last few decades, imported European warmbloods have flooded the U.S. equine market. The warmblood group includes numerous different breeds, most of whom are named for the specific regions in Europe where they originated. They have been carefully selected for centuries for their kind temperaments, rideability, and talent for English sports (dressage, jumping, and driving).

Generally taller than Quarter Horses and bigger-bodied than Thoroughbreds, warmbloods and warmblood crosses are now being bred in the United States as well. Some of the more popular breeds include **Hanoverians**, **Oldenburgs**, **Trakehners**, **Holsteiners** (all from Germany), the **Selle Français** (from France), and **Swedish and Dutch Warmbloods**.

Pedigree Research

A horse's pedigree—or family tree—can tell you a lot about his potential in a particular sport. For example, if his parents and grandparents were all champion cutting horses, chances are he'll have some cutting talent. If he comes from a long line of distance runners, he may have the talent for endurance or eventing.

Thanks to ever-improving computer databases, you may be able to discover quite a lot about your new horse's heritage. If he's registered with a breed association, it'll be fairly easy to obtain his full pedigree, as well as information about his relatives' competition records. (For instance, The Jockey Club, through www.equineline.com, can supply full pedigrees and race records of any registered Thoroughbred for a nominal fee.) Otherwise, ask his former owner to supply whatever information he or she can about your horse's parents and relatives.

Chapter 11

Where to Look for a Horse

Buying a horse is a tremendous commitment, so don't give in to spur-of-the-moment temptations. Most bargain sales are cheap for a reason. Take your instructor or another knowledgeable, reliable friend along on your shopping trips to help you avoid making an impulse purchase that you might regret later.

Breeders and Trainers

If you're looking for a particular breed of horse, spend some time at breed shows and consult the national breed organization to find names of reputable breeders. In many cases, a breeder can show you some of a young horse's relatives to give you an idea of how he may develop and perform. Breeders offer mostly young stock for sale, however, and may not have older, more experienced horses suitable for your current skill level.

Many professional trainers, on the other hand, offer mature, experienced horses for sale. Trainers usually specialize in particular disciplines, and they may even show their sale horses at competitions to prove their performance abilities. Keep in mind who is in the saddle when you're watching these horses at shows. Just because a professional can win ribbons on a horse doesn't mean you'll be able to produce the same performance on that animal. A better way to evaluate a horse is to see him perform for a rider with experience and skills similar to yours.

Horse Dealers

Horse dealers concentrate primarily on buying and selling horses. In some cases, this can make the selection process easier for you. A dealer with a large sales barn will have many more horses for you to try. Good dealers often have a knack for finding a suitable horse for each rider's individual needs, but because horses come and go so frequently through their barns, they tend to know less about the horses' individual histories and personalities. Try to find a dealer with a good reputation among other riders and trainers.

Professional trainers and horse dealers can help you narrow your choices when trying to find the best horse for you.

Auctions

Horse auctions range in quality from bargain sales to "select" sales. The latter offer the crème de la crème of a particular breed, usually commanding higher-than-average prices. (The most expensive Thoroughbred ever sold at public auction was Seattle Dancer, who sold for $13.1 million at the 1985 Keeneland July Select Yearling Sale.) Unfortunately, lower-quality auctions are often frequented by meat buyers—people who buy cheap horses to sell to slaughterhouses. Many special horses have been saved from slaughter by kind people who bid them up above the going price of meat. If you do decide to go this route, arm yourself with as much research as you can—and bring along a trustworthy expert.

Answering Ads

Horses are often advertised online, in equine magazines and local newspapers, and at tack and feed stores. Finding the right horse through ads requires a certain skill in "reading between the lines." For example, when an ad reads, "not for beginner," it may be implying that the horse bucks, rears, or is otherwise too dangerous for an amateur. A "bombproof" horse, on the other hand, is usually quiet and safe, but may also be lazy and untalented.

Beware of claims made about various talents, too. For example, a horse who "jumps four feet" may do so easily on his own (i.e., jumping over his pasture fence) but may not necessarily have the training to carry a beginner rider safely over jumps. Here are some other common words that are good to know:

Packer – Experienced horse, usually safe for beginners.

Made – Trained, experienced. (A "made" horse who has spent years competing on the show circuit is usually

Caveat emptor (Buyer Beware)

This is the best advice you'll ever get when looking for a new horse. Like any other salesmen, horse dealers will try to show you only their horses' positive qualities. Drugging sale horses to disguise soundness or behavioral problems is not uncommon. Even honest horse sellers, in an effort to make a match work, may unwittingly mislead you about a horse's qualities or neglect to disclose his faults and idiosyncrasies. The more you know about the seller, the better. You may be lucky enough to find a "diamond in the rough" through a random newspaper ad, but if you really want to know what you're getting, go to a reputable breeder or horse dealer who has a long list of satisfied customers.

worth more than less-seasoned horses.)

Push-button – Easy to ride.

Easy keeper – Requires little feed and hay to maintain his ample waistline.

No vices – Doesn't bite, kick, buck, etc. (Since almost any horse can be provoked to behave out of character, these claims shouldn't be considered absolute guarantees.)

Spooky – Opposite of bombproof: easily startles at unexpected sights and sounds (and sometimes at nothing at all), potentially trampling nearby human toes and dislodging unprepared riders from the saddle.

Green or green-broke – Relatively inexperienced. In different sports, "green" can have different meanings. For example, in the show hunters, a green horse may be in his first or second year of jumping courses in competition. A green-broke western horse, on the other hand, has been under saddle only a handful of times. Green horses are not appropriate mounts for beginners in any discipline.

Schoolmaster – A horse, usually middle-aged or older, with a great deal of experience and training. In dressage, this term often refers to retired upper-level performers.

Schoolhorse – A horse ridden by students in riding lessons. School horses don't necessarily have the advanced training and skills of schoolmasters.

Serviceably sound – Usually describes a horse who has a minor soundness problem, such as arthritis, which may need special attention (medication, etc.), but won't prohibit him from low-level activity.

TB – Thoroughbred

TBx – Thoroughbred cross (mixed breed)

AQH or QH – American Quarter Horse

Evaluating Videotapes

Requesting a videotape of a sale horse that's not within easy driving distance can save you a lot of time and trouble. Ask that the video show the horse standing still (without tack, blankets, bandages, etc.) from both sides, the front, and back. It should then show the horse walk, trot, and canter—in both directions—under saddle. Anything else the owner claims the horse can do—jump, rope, race barrels, etc.—should be demonstrated on the tape. Don't be afraid to ask the seller to zoom in on specific areas you want to see. Remember, you're the customer!

Although a professional trainer or breeder may be able to make a decision to buy a horse based on the video and the horse's and seller's reputations, this isn't advisable for lower-level riders. Just as you wouldn't buy a car you haven't driven, don't buy a horse you haven't ridden. Show the video to your instructor and, if she likes what she sees, arrange to have her accompany you on a "test drive".

Everybody Wants a Cut!

If you've received help from trainers, dealers, and other experts while choosing your new horse, you may find yourself having to pay for more than just the agreed-upon purchase price. Many experts (except veterinarians, who charge standard fees for their services) request a commission for assisting in a sale.

Before you head out with your experts to try a horse, discuss their rates and be sure you're prepared to pay them. It's not unusual for two or more people involved in the same sale to demand compensation. Make it very clear to all parties involved that you plan to pay only one commission.

As you probably know, you can buy just about anything on the Internet these days—including a horse! Various Web sites exist to connect buyers and sellers of horses of all ages, sizes, breeds, and disciplines. As convenient as this sounds, don't let the ease of the Internet replace the actual process of seeing and trying a horse in person. Nothing is riskier than buying a horse "sight unseen."

Finding Your Horse Online

You should be able to evaluate all aspects of a potential horse's abilities before making a decision.

Chapter 12

The Final Selection

If you're a true horse lover, you may fall for the first horse you try. That's normal. Horses are beautiful, wonderful creatures and most of them are hard to resist. Sometimes it's just the look in a horse's eye that draws you to him—a noble "look of eagles" or a gentle curiosity. It's important to buy a horse who appeals to you, but try not to let your emotions override more practical considerations. Take time to get to know the horse before you let yourself fall for him—and try out (ride and evaluate) several horses before making your final decision.

When you first meet a new horse, ask the owner as many questions as you can about his background and personality. Unfortunately, not all owners will answer honestly and thoroughly. Try to glean as much information as possible from the answers you receive and, when in doubt, ask an expert for a second opinion. A seller who really cares about the horse's future should also ask you about your background to decide if this will be a good match.

Ground Manners

Your new horse's ground manners—the way he behaves around you when you're leading, grooming, and saddling him—are as important as his behavior under saddle. When you go to evaluate a horse, be sure to arrive in time to watch him being saddled and led to the arena, and stick around after the ride to watch how he acts while being unsaddled and put away.

Just like kids, not all horses are born with wonderful manners. Youngsters can be unruly, disrespectful, and sometimes even dangerous (although they don't necessarily mean to be). With calm, expert handling, almost all horses can be taught good ground manners. But, in the hands of an inexperienced, nervous, and/or less assertive person, young horses can develop very bad habits. All horses' ground manners need consistent reinforcement, but your first horse shouldn't need any retraining when you buy him.

A horse with good ground manners should stand quietly while tied and walk respectfully next to his handler's side while being led. Occasional spooks (startling at unexpected sights or sounds) are normal and forgivable in most horses, but one who spooks frequently or who jumps dramatically one way or another is probably not suitable. Good horses essentially learn to spook in place—so they neither trample their handlers' feet nor dump their riders.

The "Test Drive"

Before you buy a horse, it's very important to find out whether or not you'll be compatible riding partners. Arrange a time with the seller when you can try the horse under saddle—and show up ready to ride (i.e., in boots and riding pants,

This horse has excellent ground manners!

carrying your safety helmet, gloves, etc.). Before you get on, insist that the owner or someone else familiar with the horse ride him first. This way you not only get to watch how he performs, but you also avoid being the "guinea pig" on a strange horse.

Watch as she mounts. Does the horse stand still? Ask the rider to show you everything that you would like to do with him. For instance, if you hope to jump him some day, even if you're not ready to jump yet yourself, ask her to demonstrate his jumping skills. Meanwhile, ask as many questions as you can about the horse's experience and attitude under saddle.

Before you get on the horse, ask the owner for advice on

143

It may help for your instructor or expert friend to ride the horse as well, to get a feel for his suitability. If you can't accomplish everything you'd hoped for in this first ride, ask the seller if you can return another day to try the horse again. Sometimes it's easier to judge a horse's compatibility after you've had a little time to get to know him. It also may help to see him in different environments—at other barns, at shows, on trail rides, etc.

how to ride this specific horse. Then take your time getting to know him. Not all horses will respond the same way to your "aids"—the cues you give with your legs, reins, weight shifts, and voice. Some may be more or less sensitive than the schoolhorses you're used to riding in lessons. So, test each horse's "gas pedal" and "brakes" as soon as you're mounted. Be sure you're absolutely comfortable with his "buttons" at the walk before you move on to the trot and canter.

If your instructor is with you, treat the test drive as a lesson, seeing how the horse fits into your current program. Don't try anything you haven't done before in your riding lessons, even if the owner encourages you to do so. Stay in your comfort zone. Test out your skills on him in the arena first. Then, if there's a safe place to ride outside the ring and you've had experience doing it, ask if you can test him out in the open. (If he spooks or acts in any way that makes you uncomfortable in the ring, don't risk taking him outside.) Even better, ask if the owner or another rider at the stable can accompany you on a quiet horse on a trail ride. This will give you a good feel for how this new horse behaves away from home.

Trial Period

In some circumstances, a seller may be willing to let you take the horse on trial for a week or two. To protect both parties, write up a contract clarifying all of the responsibilities you're accepting in this deal (paying veterinary and farrier bills, board, insurance, etc.) and the financial terms of the deal (for example, note whether or not the deposit you pay the owner is refundable)—and be sure the owner signs the document. During the trial period, plan to take plenty of lessons, trail rides, etc., to

A safe place to "test drive" a horse you're considering is in an indoor arena.

see how this horse fits into your life.

Another alternative may be to lease the horse with an option to buy. This is a great way to get your toes wet before taking the big plunge into horse ownership. Again, be sure to write up and have the owner sign a comprehensive contract.

Prepurchase Veterinary Exam

Before finalizing the sale, arrange to have a veterinarian perform a prepurchase exam on the horse. If possible, hire somebody who is familiar with the discipline in which you intend to ride. Depending on how thorough you want it to be, a prepurchase exam can cost anywhere from $100

Drug Testing

In some cases, you may opt to have the horse drug tested. Your veterinarian can test for medications that may be masking an injury or lameness and for tranquilizers or sedatives that may make him appear calmer and more rideable than he normally is. Older, arthritic horses are often shown and maintained on low levels of anti-inflammatory medications, such as phenylbutazone, or "bute." Horses sold at auction may also be medicated or sedated for various reasons. If you, your instructor, or your veterinarian have any doubt about whether or not the horse you intend to purchase is drug free, request a drug test.

to $800 or more. The cheapest version is a head-to-tail physical evaluation. The veterinarian looks for signs of illness, unsoundness (lameness), and past injuries that may affect the horse's ability to serve your purposes.

No horse is perfect and no veterinarian can guarantee a horse's future health and soundness, but the discoveries he makes can help influence your decision on whether or not to buy the horse. To provide a fuller picture of the horse's current health or to answer any questions about his history, he may suggest doing additional tests (x-rays, endoscopic exam, nuclear scan, bloodwork, etc.—ask your veterinarian to explain their purposes). These tests can add significantly to the exam price, so decide ahead of time how much you're willing to spend.

When Friends on the Ground Don't Click Under Saddle

Sadly, not every horse you fall in love with in the barnyard is going to be a suitable mount for you. Some horses with wonderful, lovable personalities on the ground can be surprisingly quirky or challenging to get along with under saddle. Even nicely trained, experienced horses may not click with certain types of riders. For example, some horses don't respond well to riders with "electric legs" (who unwittingly encourage horses to go faster and faster) or to strong, forceful riders. Others may perform poorly for tentative, less demanding riders. There's not always an obvious reason for why a horse and rider will or won't click. Keep this in mind when you're horse shopping.

It's important that a veterinarian examine any horse you're considering buying, paying particular attention to past injuries or potential lameness as well as overall health.

Top 15 Questions to Ask the Seller

1. How old is the horse? (Horses older than about five years are best for beginner riders.)
2. How long have you owned/known him?
3. Has he been ridden by a professional or an amateur?
4. How many years of training has he had?
5. How are his manners around the barn?
6. What kinds of things spook him?
7. Has he shown in competition before? If so, how did he do?
8. What type of rider does he get along with best? (Your riding instructor can help evaluate what kind of rider you are.)
9. How does he behave in the company of other horses?
10. How does he behave when he's out in the open and when he's away from other horses?
11. What health issues has he had?
12. How does he trailer (load, unload, stand tied)?
13. How much exercise does he need (under saddle and/or out in the pasture)?
14. What are his particular shoeing and nutritional needs?
15. How does he behave around small children, dogs, etc.?

Part 4

Preparing for Your Horse

Chapter 13

Home, Sweet Home

One of the most important things to ask
yourself before bringing a horse into your life
is: "Where will he live?" If you have a large
enough backyard (one to two acres per horse
is the general rule of thumb), keeping him
at home may be an option. Otherwise, you'll
have to find a local boarding facility that suits
your budget and standards. Both situations
have their pros and cons.

*H*aving your horse at home gives you a chance to bond with him and make him a part of the family. Boarding may cost more, but it relieves you of the day-to-day horse-care responsibilities that demand so much time and commitment (requiring you, for example, to line up a reliable "horse-sitter" every time you have to work late or leave town). If you don't have much experience caring for horses, consider boarding your horse at a reputable, professional facility for a period of time before bringing him home. You can learn a great deal about horse care by observing and talking with the barn manager, staff, and other boarders.

Home Away From Home: Boarding

Take time to select a boarding facility that meets your needs and standards. Depending on where you live and what your budget is, you may have to make some compromises. In general, though, you should feel comfortable about the quality of care your horse will be getting.

Full-care board, which can range from about $250 to more than $1,000 per month, usually includes feeding (hay and grain at least twice a day), stall mucking, and turn-out (free time in a paddock or pasture). It does not cover veterinary or shoeing expenses. Some boarding facilities offer extra services, such as grooming, blanketing, and training, for additional fees. Be sure you understand what your monthly board bill will and will not include before you commit to moving your horse in.

When evaluating a boarding facility, look closely at the horses there. Do they look healthy, happy, and well fed? Is the barn clean and tidy? Are the stalls and fencing in good repair? Will your horse get adequate turn-out (a minimum of two or three hours—preferably more—per day)? Ask other boarders how they feel about the quality of care their horses receive.

Since you'll probably be spending a great deal of time at this facility, it's also important that you enjoy the company of the staff and other

If you're a first-time horse owner, it's very important that you feel confident about the people who will be responsible for your horse. It's also essential that the barn staff members are accessible throughout the day and willing to provide the answers, advice, and moral support you're sure to require.

boarders. Wonderfully fun and supportive communities exist at many boarding stables. Finding the one that suits your personality—as well as your horse's—is all part of the process.

If you choose to board your horse, make sure you're very comfortable with all aspects of the barn and environment.

Although some barns are open to riders of multiple disciplines, it's often easier for beginners to board at barns that primarily focus on their sport of choice. The best-case situation is a facility with one or more qualified resident instructors from whom you can take lessons. It's much easier to schedule lessons with an instructor who won't have to travel to your barn or won't require you to trailer to hers. It's also beneficial to have an instructor nearby to answer questions and help you solve unexpected problems.

Riding Arena

As you're learning, it's important to ride in a safely enclosed arena with level footing. If you live in a colder climate and plan to train through the winter, you'll also want access to an indoor arena. Riding in the snow can be great fun, but trying to do any serious training on unpredictable footing is nearly impossible—-and sometimes unsafe. So, plan to find a place with an indoor arena or be prepared to "let your horse down" over the winter.

Ask the staff at each potential boarding facility how many riders use the ring and at what times of the day. Heavy arena traffic can be difficult for beginner riders to navigate and can make scheduling lessons complicated. You may be more comfortable at a facility with large and/or multiple arenas.

Access to Trails

Trail riding is one of the most enjoyable things you can do with your horse. As open lands across the country rapidly succumb to development pressures, "bridle paths" are growing scarcer and scarcer. If you plan to trail ride, whether or not you'll have access to open land should be a deciding factor in where you choose to keep your horse. Although there's nothing better than being able to hit the trail right out of your own backyard, you may have to compromise and locate your horse somewhere within easy trailering distance to good trails.

Many national and local organizations are working to preserve open lands and keep them accessible to horse riders. If trail riding is important to you, try to get involved with one of these groups. Formore information, contact the Equestrian Land Conservation Resource, www.elcr.org.

Before you ride on any trail, find out first if it is privately or publicly owned and if it's open to horses. Even if a small section of the trail crosses private property, be sure to ask the owner's permission to ride on it. The better respect we all show both private and public landowners, the longer their trails will be kept open to horse people.

A Stable (at) Home
Horse-Friendly Neighbors

If you decide to keep your horse at home, first check whether or not it's legal to do so. Some neighborhood zoning laws restrict the types of livestock residents can keep on their property. Consult your town or county planning board to find out if horses are allowed in your area. If you belong to a homeowner's association, you'll need to get approval from the other homeowners as well.

Share your plans with your neighbors. Horses add to the noise, dust,

and odor levels in the area. They can also be a danger to children and pets trespassing onto your property. (In most states, horses are known as an attractive nuisance and their owners are legally responsible for injuries they cause to others, even trespassers.) On the other hand, if your barn and pasture are attractively built and maintained, your horse operation actually may add to your neighbors' property value. These are all good issues to discuss with your neighbors before bringing a horse onto your property.

Consider it a real bonus if your barn has access to trails, and get out on them as frequently as possible.

Shelter

One of the most important things you need to provide for your horse is shelter from the elements. Wind, rain, snow, and the heat of the sun can all take their toll on a horse's comfort and health. Horses are especially vulnerable to strong winds, which ruffle their hairs and penetrate their insulating winter coats. The worst combination—cold wind and precipitation—can easily chill a horse, making him susceptible to illness.

A solid, three-sided run-in shed that's wide enough for your horse to

Finding a "home" for everything in your barn can make your life a lot easier. Tack and equipment, for example, will stay cleaner and last longer if you store it in a room or closet. Grain should always be stored in a clean, rodent-proof container in a cool, dry place that your horse can't access if he manages to escape his stall or paddock. (Many horses will literally eat themselves sick if they get into the grain supply.) Hay should be stored off of the ground and sheltered from rain and snow. If possible, store it in a separate building near the barn. This will reduce fire danger and, in some states, may even lower your property insurance premium.

turn around and lie down in comfortably and deep enough for him to get completely out of the weather is ideal. If you have a barn, or plan to build one, be sure to provide enough stalls for the number of horses you'll have—about 12-by-12-feet is a good size for the average horse. There are many other horse-specific needs to take into consideration when building a barn (including location, drainage, flooring, materials, etc.), so consult knowledgeable horse people before you start building.

Horse-Proofing the Barnyard

The combination of swift reflexes and naturally flighty natures makes horses inherently accident-prone. Almost every horse owner has, at some time or another, had to call a veterinarian to stitch up a wound caused by a horse either running into something or getting kicked by a pasturemate. Many such accidents are inevitable; however, there's a lot you can do to minimize the risk of them happening to your horse.

Start by horse-proofing your barnyard (or, if you're boarding, carefully inspecting the boarding facility) before bringing him home. Remove all dangerous objects, such as nails, metal, sharp edges of feeders, etc. Replace any protruding hooks, cabinet handles, etc., on which your horse might catch his halter or poke an eye, with spring-type latches and round and/or flexible hooks (available in some horse-supply catalogs), etc. Stow pitchforks, brooms, and other equipment away from areas where you lead or tie your horse. In general, the less clutter there is around your barnyard, the safer it will be.

Be especially cautious about electric wires and devices in your barnyard. Horses can easily electrocute themselves by chewing on an exposed wire or cutting through an extension cord with a horseshoe. All electric outlets in the barn should be located well out of every horse's reach. Fans, electric water heaters, and other devices should be installed in such a way that minimizes risk of electrocution. When you use electrical appliances—clippers, vacuum, etc.—around your horse, be vigilant about keeping the cords safely clear of his teeth and hooves.

Ventilation and Lighting

Good ventilation in a barn is essential to your horse's health. Respiratory problems are prevalent in warm, closed-up stables, but rare in ones that provide cross-ventilation via windows or vents from all four sides. Ceiling and ventilator fans can help increase air circulation as well, as can bars between horses' stalls. In warm climates, high ceilings help improve air circulation and keep a barn cool.

The importance of good lighting in a barn is also often underestimated. Well-lit barns are easier and safer to work in and less likely to attract flies. To keep your electricity costs down, install windows and skylights wherever possible and paint the insides of your barn white.

Room to Roam

In their natural state, horses wander and graze for most of the day. Being confined to a stall is highly unnatural for them. So, the best thing you can do for your horse's physical and mental health is to provide him with plenty of pasture or "turn-out" time.

Fencing

Fencing is a necessary evil in the horse world. We need it to keep horses safe and separate from others, but it has two major drawbacks: First, no matter how sturdy and well-designed it is, all fencing fails at some point—opening the door for horses to escape. Second, horses can—and do—injure themselves on even the most carefully placed and maintained fences. Their curious and flighty nature simply makes them prone to pawing at, rubbing on, or running into man-made barriers.

Depending on where you live, traditional wooden fencing may be an option, but it's sure to require a great deal of maintenance over the years. In the long run, it may be cheaper to install electric fencing or a more durable, synthetic fencing made specifically for horses. One of the safest and most effective options, the former can be used either on its own or in conjunction with a traditional fence. A highly visible (braided rope or synthetic tape), well-grounded electric fence not only protects horses from injuring themselves on solid fencing, but also reduces maintenance costs resulting from chewing and rubbing.

Some wire-mesh fencing made specifically for horses can be acceptable, too. Be sure the holes in the wire are not big enough for your horse to get his hoof through.

Smart Coats

Sub-zero temperatures? No problem for horses! As winter approaches, their coats naturally grow longer and thicker, making them resemble wooly mammoths. When the temperature drops, tiny muscles attached to the roots of the long coat hairs, called pilorector muscles, contract. This causes the long hairs to stand up on end, trapping an insulating layer of warm air around your horse's body. Snow, mud, and manure can mat the long hairs down, inhibiting this pilorection mechanism, so it's important to groom your horse's coat regularly throughout the winter.

Whatever fencing you choose, make a habit of checking the fenceline regularly, to discover broken sections or electrical shortages before your horse does. This extra effort on your part will be well worth the potential tragedies that could result from a breakaway (particularly in heavily trafficked areas where a loose horse could be hit by a car).

Forage

The best pastures contain enough grass cover to keep horses busily grazing throughout the day. The grass need not be lush—in fact, extremely lush grass can upset the systems of some horses, and many ponies—but, ideally, it should be relatively weed-free and hardy enough to stand up to hoof traffic.

The most effective way to maintain a healthy pasture is to divide it into separate sections and rotate horses through them every few days. Regular mowing will help minimize weeds. To recover bare spots and fortify heavily trafficked areas, ask your local farm-supply store to recommend the best seed varieties for your particular region and climate. Your agricultural extension agent can provide advice about seed varieties, liming, and other pasture-management techniques, as well.

Pasture Dangers

Before turning your horse out into a new pasture or leading him past your newly landscaped lawn, be sure he won't be tempted to munch on any **poisonous plants**. Certain naturally occurring trees, weeds, and flowers, as well as some ornamental bushes and plants used for gardens and landscaping, can be toxic to horses. See the Resources section for more information. **Barbed wire** should never be used as fencing for horses. The sharp barbs can cause serious, sometimes fatal injuries. Even horses raised in barbed-wire fenced pasture or trained to be "wire savvy" (taught to stand still when their legs are tangled in ropes, for example) are at risk of stepping accidentally onto a loose wire or being pushed by another horse into a fence. Many veteran cow horses and "dude" horses living in barbed-wire fenced pastures bear thick scars to prove this. Furthermore, the toll that barbed wire takes on wildlife (deer, moose, elk, etc.) is impossible to measure, but we can assume that it's devastating.

Assembling Your Support Team

No matter how hands-on you are in your horse's care, you won't be able to guarantee him the best health and happiness without the support of a team of professionals. Since fees vary from one expert to another, your budget may play a large role in your choices. However, keep in mind that you often get what you pay for—sometimes you have to pay a little extra for good-quality care. In each case, thoroughly research the expert's background, character, and credentials before making a final decision about him or her.

Barn Manager and Staff

If you board your horse, the people you're going to rely on the most will be the barn manager and staff. These are the people who see your horse day after day—during feeding time, while mucking his stall, while bringing him to and from the pasture, etc. Depending on your boarding situation, they may also be the people who provide any special care, such as blanketing and medication. Consequently, they'll probably be the first to notice any

Dust Is Trouble

Ventilation is especially important in dusty barns: The dustier your barn, the more airborne particles entering and potentially damaging your horse's lungs. Even on very cold days, it's healthiest to open up doors and windows and circulate out the bad air, so long as the air is still. Remember, too much wind can be unhealthy, too, so try to minimize excessive drafts.

Safety and durability are two of the most important factors to consider when selecting fencing material.

changes in his behavior or health. This is very important, because the sooner an injury or illness is identified, the more easily and effectively it can be treated.

At a good boarding stable, the manager and staff should make the well-being of the horses their number-one priority. Be sure they know how to contact you in the case of an emergency. Whenever you leave town, give them the phone numbers of where you'll be staying.

Veterinarian

From the outset, you're going to want to know that you have a reliable, skilled equine veterinarian on call to answer your questions and respond to emergencies. Ideally, he or she should be located within about a 20-minute drive. Even if you don't experience veterinary emergencies, you will need to make regular appointments for your horse's annual vaccinations, checkups, and health certificates (required by law whenever you travel across state lines). Some veterinarians work alone and some work in multi-person practices. In either case, be sure that the veterinarian you choose provides a 24-hour emergency service.

Some boarding facilities already have a vet and farrier on call who make regular visits for all of the horses in the barn. Discuss with the stable manager what routine care you'll be responsible for scheduling and what care is given to all of the horses as part of the boarding program.

Farrier

Besides your instructor, the professional you'll probably spend the most time with (and the most money on) is your farrier, or blacksmith. Horses' hooves grow constantly, just like your fingernails. If they grow too long or wear unevenly, they can make your horse uncomfortable or even lame. To prevent this from happening, your farrier should trim, balance and, if necessary, shoe your horse every four to six weeks. Ask your instructor or veterinarian to recommend a qualified, reliable farrier.

Equine Dentist

As I'll explain in Chapter 21, your horse will need regular dental care also. Designed to wear away gradually as he eats a normal diet of grains and grasses, his teeth grow continually throughout his lifetime. The way they meet when he chews creates sharp edges that can cause cheek and gum pain. It's important to regularly smooth out these edges (a process called "floating") and treat any other dental problems. The best person for this job is a qualified veterinarian or certified equine dental technician.

Family

Last, but not least, you're going to need the support of your family. This doesn't necessarily mean that your parents will be out mucking stalls with you at 5 a.m. or that your spouse will tack your horse up for your lessons. The most you can ask of your family members is that they try to understand your commitment and responsibility to your horse. And, especially if they're not interested in horses themselves, you need to understand the inconveniences your hobby will add to their lives.

Horses can be addictive and incredibly time-consuming. Be careful not to unconsciously compromise your family's needs for your equestrian goals. If you're fair, patient, and willing to give up an occasional ride to be with your family members, they'll eventually learn to accept your new passion—even if they don't entirely understand it.

Because the health of your horse's feet is so critical, your farrier (or blacksmith) is someone you will need to trust completely.

Chapter 14

Your Horse's Paperwork

Okay, so you've found the

horse of your dreams and

the perfect place for him to live.

Now are you ready to bring him home?

Not quite. There are a few final details

you need to take care of.

Health Records

Before handing over any money for your new four-legged friend, ask the former owner for complete written records of the horse's health history. Ideally, these will include everything from minor injuries to serious ailments and lamenesses. The more you and your veterinarian know about his past health, the better you'll be able to maintain his health in the future.

Vaccination and De-worming History

Ask the former owner which diseases your horse has been vaccinated against and when he received his last vaccinations. Also ask when he was most recently de-wormed and which brand of de-wormer he was given. In Chapter 21, I'll explain the importance of vaccination and de-worming and will tell you how to incorporate them into your new horse's health care program.

Coggins Test

In certain situations, particularly if the horse will be crossing state lines following the sale, state laws require that the horse changing hands be tested for Equine Infectious Anemia, or swamp fever. This highly contagious, fatal disease has no cure or vaccine, but can be identified in infected horses by a blood test, called a Coggins test. Different states have different requirements about how frequently horse owners should perform Coggins tests on their animals (every 6 to 12 months is typical). Ask your veterinarian if your new horse will need a current Coggins test to make his bill of sale legal.

Identification Papers

When a horse changes hands, various documents usually accompany him in the transaction. No sale should be considered final without a written bill of sale, signed by both the buyer and seller. If the horse is registered with a breed association, ask the seller to transfer his registration papers to you. Upper-level sport horses may have an FEI passport (administered by the Fédération Equestre Internationale), which is required in many international competitions.

Feeding Instructions

One of the many basic-care details you'll want to ask your horse's former owner about is specific feeding instructions. How much grain does he eat and what brand of grain is he fed? How much and what kind of hay does he eat? (For both hay and grain, ask for exact amounts, measured in weight, not volume.) How often is he fed? As I'll explain in Chapter 18, horses are very sensitive to sudden changes in their diets. During this time of transition, keeping him on his regular feeding schedule will help minimize undue stress on his system.

Shoeing History

Ask how often your new horse has been shod or, if he's barefoot, how often his feet have been trimmed in the past. When was he last shod? Does he have any special shoeing requirements? If you plan to use the same farrier who cared for your horse previously, he'll probably already know all of this essential information. However, if you'll be hiring a farrier who's not familiar with your horse, any information you can share will help him or her to maintain your horse's future comfort and soundness.

Special Care

Before you take your horse home, pick the seller's brain one last time. Ask, "Is there anything else I should know about him?" Sometimes even the littlest details can help

If possible, keep your new horse on the diet to which he was accustomed, as horses are sensitive to sudden changes.

make your—and your horse's—life easier. For example, he may like being turned out to pasture in the mornings but may get anxious and start to walk up and down the fenceline if you leave him out past feeding time. Or, he may have a particular skin sensitivity that requires extra grooming or washing. The list of potential equine quirks and demands is endless.

Insurance

Another thing to consider before you sign the bill of sale is an equine insurance policy. Not only might this protect your investment, it may also help you cover unexpected health- and accident-related expenses. Insurance agencies and companies specializing in equine policies advertise in horse magazines and on the Internet. Here are the typical services they offer:

Mortality Policy

This covers death caused by accident, injury, or illness. Premium rates range between about three and four percent of a horse's value, depending on his age, breed, and discipline (jumpers, for example, usually have higher rates than dressage horses). Companies offer these policies for horses between the ages of about 6 months and 18 years. (Some will also cover young foals and horses older than 18, but at much higher rates.) They also reserve the right to exclude preexisting conditions and to deny coverage to horses deemed unsound or unhealthy.

Endorsements

Once you buy a mortality policy, you can opt to add endorsements, such as:

Major-medical — covers medical and surgical procedures

required to treat illness, injury, or disease.

Surgical-only — just covers operating room charges and aftercare medical expenses.

Loss-of-use or permanent-disability — requires the company to reimburse you for a percentage (usually between 50 and 75 percent) of your horse's value if an injury, accident, or illness renders him permanently and completely unable to perform the use specified in the policy.

If you do decide to purchase insurance coverage for your horse, here are a few quick tips:

★ Check that the company underwriting the policy is a "licensed" or "admitted" carrier in your state, with a good financial rating.

★ Review the policy wording with your agent and be sure all of the agreed-upon terms are clearly written in it.

★ Learn the company's notification protocol and be sure you know whom you are required to contact in the case of an emergency or claim. Post that person's phone number and your horse's policy number in his stable.

Liability

The combination of today's litigious society and the unpredictable nature of horses makes horse owners particularly vulnerable to lawsuits. If your horse injures someone else or harms someone's property, that person may sue you to cover medical expenses, repairs, etc. In some cases, your homeowner's policy may protect you. (If it does, confirm with your agent that you're covered even when your horse is off your property.) However, more comprehensive, equine-specific policies are available. Ask your equine insurance specialist to discuss the various available options with you.

Horses From Other States and Countries

In some U.S. states, horse ownership must be verified by an official brand inspector. When you buy a new horse, the seller should transfer his brand inspection certificate to you. This means that he or she will need to contact the local brand inspector to complete the paperwork.

Horses imported from other countries may also have documented passports.

Endorsements don't cover preventative/maintenance expenses, such as vaccinations, checkups, etc. And not all horses are eligible for every type of coverage.

Preventing Horse Theft

Sadly, a number of horses around the country are stolen from their stables and pastures every year. Some of these horses are recovered, but many disappear forever. Thieves sell them on to unwitting buyers in private transactions, at auctions, and even take them to slaughterhouses. Here are a few things you can do to protect your horse from this fate:

★ Ask your veterinarian about permanent identification methods, such as tattoos, freeze-branding, and microchips.

★ At night, pasture or stable your horse close to the house and far from busy roads.

★ Consider locking gates and installing other types of security systems on your property.

★ Pay attention to suspicious-looking passersby and visitors.

★ If your horse disappears, immediately contact your local police department and state veterinarian. If you suspect that he's been stolen (and hasn't simply escaped on his own), recruit helpers to contact the closest horse auctions and slaughterhouses.

Left: To be sure you and your horse spend many happy, healthy years together, consider purchasing a mortality policy with a major medical endorsement.

Chapter 15

Tools of the Trade

The first time you wander through a tack shop or page through a horse-products catalog, you might be a little overwhelmed by how many different things you can buy for your four-legged friend. You will need to buy several basic pieces of equipment and tack (saddle, bridle, etc.), but much of this is optional. If you're into fashion, the good news is that most horse products these days are available in a rainbow of colors, so color-coordinate away!

Around the Barn

Halters and Lead Ropes

The most basic pieces of equipment you'll need are a halter and lead shank. Halters are available in leather, nylon, and rope. A nonbreakable nylon or rope halter can be dangerous if your horse catches it on something or falls down while he's tied, for example, in the trailer. Many people prefer to use a leather halter or a nylon halter with a leather crownpiece (the part that goes behind your horse's ears), which will break under extreme pressure.

In some cases, however, you might not want the halter to break. For example, if your horse develops a bad habit of pulling backward when he's tied up, he'll probably do it more often if he knows he can break free. Switching to a nonbreakable halter just when he's tied under supervision may discourage him from pulling back. Be sure to remove the halter or replace it with a breakable one before turning him loose in his stall or pasture.

When leading your horse, should he suddenly try to pull away, a nylon lead shank can give your hands rope burns. Instead, buy soft cotton lead ropes. (Leather shanks are fine, too, but they're not as easy to tie as cotton ropes.) A shank with a chain on the end may be useful for controlling horses with poor ground manners, but, if used improperly, can be abusive. If you think a chain shank is necessary, ask your instructor to show you how to attach and use it correctly. Never tie a horse with a chain shank attached over his nose, and never double a chain shank through the halter and back to itself—this creates a dangerous loop in which your horse could get a hoof caught or you could injure a finger.

Your horse's halter should fit comfortably around his nose, with the noseband resting two inches below his cheekbone, just loose enough for you to fit two to three fingers underneath it. The strap around his jaw should be snug enough to keep the halter out of his eyes, but still loose enough to fit two fingers underneath it.

Stable Necessities

If you're keeping your horse at home, you'll need some basic tools, such as a **wheelbarrow** (or muck bucket), **shovel**, **broom**, and **pitchfork**. There are two kinds of pitchforks: The

A halter and lead line are absolute necessities for horses.

traditional four- to six-tined metal fork works great for shifting hay and cleaning straw-bedded stalls. A plastic or metal fork with more tines, sometimes called an apple-picker, is more effective for cleaning stalls bedded with wood shavings or sawdust. If you're boarding and want to use your own equipment, be sure it's clearly marked with your name in permanent marker.

In addition to the grooming kit described in Chapter 5, you may also want to purchase a:

Mounting block or stepstool – Unless your horse's nose only comes up to about your waist, you'll need a boost to groom his hard-to-reach areas (withers, back, behind the ears). Whether you choose a plastic mounting block (available in tack stores and catalogs), a bale of hay, or a stepstool, be sure it's stable and safe: no sharp edges, no collapsible legs, and no dangerous parts that your horse can get himself tangled up

Keep an extra halter and lead shank handy at all times. Horses are both excellent equipment saboteurs and escape artists. At some point, you'll have to grab your spare halter to replace a broken one or catch a loose horse.

in accidentally. (A mounting block is also useful for its originally intended purpose: mounting.)

Sweat scraper, sponges, and wash bucket – You'll need these for bathing your horse. A sweat scraper is a long, curved, metal or plastic tool used to scrape water off your horse (helping him cool and dry faster). Look for big, durable sponges that fit comfortably in your hand. Many horses will turn up their noses at drinking water that smells soapy, so buy at least one large bucket to use strictly for washing. To keep it separate from his drinking water buckets, buy one of a different color. For thorough washings, it's also handy to have a long hose with an attachable spray nozzle.

Vacuum – A horse vacuum (available through horse-supply catalogs and tack stores) is one of the pricier tools to consider adding to your grooming arsenal. (A cheaper, yet effective, alternative is a regular household Shop-Vac.®) Your horse may need a few days to get used to the noise and suction feel on his skin, but it'll save you loads of time in the long run.

A sturdy wheelbarrow will make the work of cleaning stalls much more efficient.

Use it to remove caked mud and ground-in dirt from his coat. Ask an experienced horse person to show you how to use it safely and properly. As with all electric devices, be very careful to keep the electric away from your horse's teeth and hooves.

Feeding Tools
Water Buckets

Your horse will need two 18- to 20-quart water buckets in his stall, placed in the corner closest to the barn hose (to make filling easier) and farthest away from his feed tub and hay. Hang them at about his chest height—high enough so he's not likely to catch a hoof in them if he paws and low enough so he can reach them without raising his head above his shoulders. Place sturdy metal screweyes into the stall wall, and then attach the buckets to them with double-ended snaps (purchase snaps and screweyes at your local hardware store).

Feed Tub & Salt Block

Hang a feed tub—or install a triangular-shaped "corner feeder"—-at the same height as your horse's water buckets. He will need access to a salt block, as well, which can either be placed in his feed tub or in a salt-block holder, attached to the wall at about his shoulder height. (All of these containers are available at tack and feed stores.)

Where to Put Hay

The healthiest place to feed your horse hay is on the ground. The natural nose-down position allows bacteria and debris to drain from his airways while he eats. However, if there's a danger of him ingesting too much sand or dirt with the hay (which can contribute to digestive problems), install a heavy rubber mat on the ground in the area where you serve his hay. Or, buy a hay net or hay bag, which can be hung from the wall slightly above chest height. Be sure the net or bag isn't low enough for your horse to paw at and get his hoof caught in (remember that a hay net will hang even lower once it's empty).

Feed Bin

In your feed room, you'll need a heavy-duty container to store grain. A metal-lined bin with a secure lid is the best defense against rodents. To measure your horse's meals accurately, buy a feed scoop or use an empty coffee can. When you first calculate how much to feed him, you'll also need a dry-weight scale to weigh the contents of your measuring scoop or coffee can, as well as to weigh his hay servings.

Eating Outside

In the pasture, you'll need a heavy-duty metal or plastic water trough, appropriately sized for your number of horses (10 to 12 gallons per horse per day). If you're feeding grain meals outside, you'll also need a rubber feed pan (which can be placed on the ground) or a feed tub mounted to the fence or run-in shed. Another option, which is particularly useful when feeding multiple horses together in a pasture, is individual nosebags. Be sure your nosebag has plenty of air holes so water will drain out if your horse dunks it in the water trough after eating. Rubber mats can be used outdoors, too, to keep hay from mixing in with sand and dirt.

Another outdoor option is to feed hay in a low trough or hay rack (be sure it doesn't have sharp edges or bars spaced so wide apart that a horse might get a foot caught between them).

Miscellaneous Tools

You'll find many uses for a pocket knife and scissors around the barn, from cutting twine on hay bales to evening out the ends of your horse's tail. Keep these in an easy-to-reach place in case of emergency (for example, to cut a lead rope or hay net if your horse gets caught in it accidentally). Other tools, such as a hammer and screwdriver, will come in handy for fixing and adjusting various things around the barn.

Tack, Tack, and More Tack!
Bridles and Bits

The type of bridle you use on your horse will depend on what discipline you're doing, what level you and your horse are, and how sensitive he is. Most bridles include a metal, rubber, or synthetic mouthpiece, called the "bit," which puts pressure on the sensitive parts of the horse's mouth. In both western and English disciplines, the basic bridle uses a simple snaffle bit attached to a single rein on each side. Bits with more precise action, such as curbs, twisted snaffles, and gags, are often used in western sports and in more advanced English training. However, these bits can be very severe, especially when in the hands of a beginner. Double bridles (which include two separate bits) and certain types of single bits require the rider to hold two sets of reins. This is another skill that beginner riders should not try to tackle.

Ask your instructor to help you select the best bit for you and your horse. Since horses have different-sized mouths, also ask your instructor to help you check that your bit isn't too small (which would pinch your horse's lips) or too big (which might allow the bit to slide through his mouth and work less effectively).

Bitless bridles, such as hackamores and bosals, are popular in some sports. These function by applying pressure on the horse's nose and poll. Although they may look milder than bridles with bits, they can be quite severe in the wrong hands. Not all sports permit bitless bridles in competition. Again, ask your instructor for advice and, if you plan to compete, consult your sport's rulebook to see what is and isn't allowed.

A heavily populated barn will also house multiple saddles, bridles, and other tack.

Girth Sensitivity

Horses with sensitive skin can develop sores, called girth galls, behind their elbows. If your horse's skin looks irritated after you remove his girth or cinch, buy a fleece girth cover to protect these areas.

If you do buy any blankets, ask the blanket dealer to explain how to measure your horse for the correct fit.

Saddle

As I mentioned earlier, the type of saddle you use depends on what discipline you plan to do. English styles include dressage (deep seat with long, fairly straight flaps); saddle seat (fairly flat seat with long, forward flaps); jumping (shallower seat with forward-cut flaps and, in many cases, padded knee rolls); and all-purpose (a combination of dressage and jumping). Although traditional saddles are made out of leather, some of today's popular saddles are made out of synthetic materials, which are more affordable and easier to clean. Be sure to get a girth or cinch long enough to reach around your horse's belly, but short enough to tighten an extra hole or two should he drop a few pounds.

Saddle Pads

Buy at least two saddle pads or blankets so you always have a backup when one gets wet or dirty. If your saddle is slightly big for your horse or slightly unbalanced, you may be able to use a specially shaped pad to correct the problem. (Ask your instructor to help you decide if this is necessary.) On the other hand, under a saddle that fits well, too much padding can create painful pressure points, which can contribute to back soreness. So, don't go overboard with extra-thick or multiple saddle pads.

Miscellaneous Tack

Many riders accessorize with other tack items. A breastplate, for instance, keeps the saddle from slipping sideways or backward, and a crupper keeps the saddle from slipping forward. Martingales, tie downs, draw reins, and other similar devices are used to keep horses from throwing their heads in the air or to set their heads and necks in a particular position. In general, such equipment should only be used in the hands of professionals or under the supervision of an experienced instructor.

Horse Clothing
Blankets

Horses are equipped with naturally functional coats that grow longer and thicker in the winter to keep them warm and shed out in the spring to make way for thinner, cooler coats. They also maintain body heat better than we do, so they can tolerate daily swings in temperatures comfortably. Under normal circumstances, your horse

Regular washing and airing out of blankets will help to prevent skin irritation and hair loss.

Beware of trainers or other riders who advise using "gadgets" (draw reins, tie-downs, German martingales, etc.) on your horse. In most instances, use of such devices is merely a quick—and often temporary—fix, and a substitute for correct training. When used by inexperienced or forceful riders, gadgets can be overly harsh and even abusive. If your trainer recommends that you use a gadget on your horse, question his or her reasons and ask if the same goals can be reached without the gadget. In general, time, patience, and correct training are far kinder and more effective tools than gadgets.

shouldn't need any additional clothing. However, if you clip his coat (see Chapter 5), you'll need to put a blanket on him in cold weather. Depending on how much the temperature varies, you may want two blankets of different weights for indoors, as well as a waterproof "turn-out" blanket (or "rug") for outdoors. If you clip the hair off of his back and hindquarters, you may also want a "quarter sheet" to place over those muscles as you start your rides.

Whether your horse is clipped or not, if you expect him to work up a heavy sweat in cold weather, you may want to purchase a sheet (a lightweight blanket) or "cooler" made of wicking material to prevent him from catching cold as he cools off.

Leg Wear

The primary reason for covering your horse's legs with boots or bandages is to protect his tendons and ligaments from injury—either from a blow by another of his legs or from an impact with an obstacle, such as a jump. In some sports, a special bandage or boot may be used to provide extra support, thus perhaps reducing the strain on some structures of the legs.

Many trainers also like to protect the legs of horses being exercised on the longe line and of young horses learning something new, like jumping. However, a well-shod, mature horse who travels naturally in such a way that his legs don't interfere with one another shouldn't require any added protection or support to perform most lower-level sports. (In some sports, such as dressage, all boots and bandages are forbidden in the competition arena.) Ask your instructor if your horse requires protective boots.

Common Boots

Galloping or splint boots – These are leather or synthetic boots secured, with buckles or Velcro, that cover the horse's lower leg from just below the knee or hock to just below the fetlock.

Open-front galloping boots, often used by show jumpers, protect the vulnerable tendons and soft tissues in the backs of the legs, but leave the fronts of the lower legs (cannon bones) uncovered.

Over-reach or "bell" boots – Rubber or synthetic boots that cover the coronet band (the top of the hoof) and bulbs of the heels.

Easy Boots (or similar brand) – Like equine overshoes, these provide great temporary protection for the hoof wall and sole while you're waiting for the farrier to arrive to replace a thrown shoe. Endurance riders also use them to protect their horses' feet on rocky trails.

Shipping boots – These thickly padded, Velcro-attached leg coverings are designed to protect a horse from injuring his legs and hooves when "shipping"—traveling by trailer, van, etc.

Common Bandages

Traditional leg bandages are usually more difficult to apply than boots. Although bandaging takes a long time to perfect, it's a good skill to have in the case of emergencies or in the absence of "quickie" shipping boots. The best way to learn is to watch an expert do it a few times, and practice under his or her supervision.

Stable, or *"standing,"* bandages – Horses recovering from a recent leg injury are often dressed with stable bandages to keep a wound clean, reduce swelling, and/or provide support to the opposite leg. These thickly padded cotton wraps, or "quilts," held in place with carefully wound bandages, usually cover the legs from the knee or hock down to below the fetlock. Horses suffering from chronic arthritis or similar ailments may be routinely wrapped in stable bandages, particularly if they stand in stalls for long periods of time.

Applied too tightly or unevenly, a boot or bandage can interfere with the circulation in your horse's leg, causing serious and potentially permanent damage. Applied too loosely, it can slip or come unwound, becoming a danger to the horse should he trip on it.

Shipping bandages – Like stable bandages, only more thickly padded and extending all the way down over the bulbs of the heels.

Exercise bandages – These provide very little padding underneath the bandage and should only be applied by experts.

First-Aid Kits (Human and Equine)

Every barn and horse trailer should be equipped with complete human and equine first-aid kits. The latter should contain Betadine solution, triple-antibiotic ophthalmic ointment, hydrogen peroxide, rubbing alcohol, scissors, adhesive tape, gauze pads, sheet cotton, nonstick dressing, and bandages of various sizes.

The equine kit should also contain an equine thermometer (with string and clip attached to secure it to the tail), a stethoscope, a watch that shows seconds (for measuring your horse's pulse and respiration rates), a tube of Banamine (ask your veterinarian for this medication, and for instructions on how and when to use it), milk of magnesia, a clean bucket to use only for cleaning wounds, clean towels, a set of four standing wraps (leg bandages), and plenty of Vetrap—a useful, self-adhesive, flexible bandage, available in a multitude of bright colors.

Fitting the Saddle Properly

A good saddle should fit both you and your horse properly. Not only does a poor fit put you in the wrong balance and interfere with your ability to ride well, but it can also cause back soreness, lameness, and performance problems in your horse. The best way to check your saddle fit or to select a new saddle is to hire a professional saddle fitter to thoroughly evaluate you and your horse. (Ask your local tack store to recommend a qualified saddle fitter or contact the Master Saddlers Association at www.mastersaddlers.com.) Here are a few things you can check on your own:

1. Holding the saddle in front of you, you shouldn't notice any asymmetry in the structure or unevenness in the padding.
2. Place the saddle on your horse without a saddle pad or girth, sliding it into position behind his withers, so the front edge of the weight-bearing portion of the saddle is about 1½" to 2" behind your horse's shoulder blades. Then, run your hand between his body and the front panels of the saddle; the pressure should feel even all the way down. Similarly, you should feel even pressure under the two parts of the saddle (also called "panels" if the saddle is English, or "bars" if it's western) that rest on the long muscles on either side of your horse's spine.
3. The saddle should be balanced on the horse so that the middle of the seat is the lowest point. If you press down on the front of the saddle, the back shouldn't "rock" or lift up.
4. With the girth attached and you sitting in the saddle, there should still be clearance between the front of the saddle and your horse's withers.
5. When you view the saddle from the rear, the panels or bars should lie flat along the back, spreading weight over as large an area as possible. The spine should be totally clear of any saddle pressure. You

will need to stand on a mounting block or stepstool directly behind your horse, at a safe distance, to view this angle. On a western saddle, you will not be able to view the space down the spine (where the "gullet" is in an English saddle), but most western saddles have enough clearance.

6. The seat of the saddle should be big enough for you to sit in without feeling pinched in front or back. You should be able to fit approximately one hand's width between the back edge of the saddle (the cantle) and your bum.

7. Your horse's attitude and way of going (freedom of movement, length of stride, etc.) shouldn't change when you compare his performance in different saddles. Any negative changes—-ears back, swishing tail, reluctance to do a particular task—-may indicate saddle discomfort.

8. When you remove the saddle, you shouldn't notice any roughed-up hairs on his back, indicating that the saddle was shifting or rubbing during the ride. You also shouldn't see any dirt marks down the center of your saddle pad, which could mean that pressure is being put on your horse's spine.

9. As your horse's body shape changes with his fitness level, so might his saddle fit. Run through the above checklist periodically.

Polo wraps are a popular type of exercise bandage used to protect the legs during training and warm-ups for competition. They should only be applied by experienced horse people and never used in extremely wet conditions (stream crossings, etc.).

Chapter 16

Shape Up!

Riding is an athletic endeavor—for both horse and rider. Whether you plan to compete or just poke along on the trails, you both need to be fit enough to do your part. Just as with any sport, a well-planned conditioning program will minimize risk of injury and maximize your chances of success. Most importantly, paying careful attention to both your and your horse's fitness levels will help you judge whether or not you're capable of safely completing a particularly long or difficult ride. Being able to recognize physical limitations is a crucial factor in preventing accidents caused by exhaustion or overfacing (attempting a challenge for which you and/or your horse aren't prepared).

Start with Yourself

Just because your horse is carrying you on his back doesn't mean he should be doing all of the work. Riding with good posture, strength, balance, flexibility, and coordination makes your horse's job easier. The better you can control your own body and balance, the more effectively you'll stay "out of your horse's way," allowing him to perform to the best of his abilities. So be fair: Make a conditioning plan for yourself before doing the same for your horse.

As with any fitness program, consult your physician before attempting anything new or before increasing your workout level dramatically. If possible, consult a physical trainer about designing a program that addresses your particular needs and goals. You can choose from a number of different types of fitness regimens to get yourself in shape for riding. Try to find one or two that you'll enjoy enough to keep up. Here are a few possibilities:

★ For aerobic fitness: walking, running, skipping rope, swimming, aerobics

★ To improve balance, strength, and flexibility: yoga, Pilates, dance

★ To improve strength: exercises (with or without weights) focusing on the upper back, lower back, abdomen, and legs. "Lunges" and "squats," for example, are great for strengthening the legs and lower back. Ask a physical trainer to show you how to do them properly.

Riding multiple horses each day is another good way to improve your fitness. However, many top riders will tell you that exercising off the horse enhances their abilities in the saddle.

If you dismount after a ride less winded and sweaty than your horse, your fitness program is working!

Evaluating Your Horse's Fitness

Is your horse flabby or fit? You may be able to tell just by looking at him. A fit horse has firm, well-defined muscles and an obviously athletic

Right: You'll find that the chores you need to do around the barn will provide you with a workout, too.

Go for Strength and Flexibility

Your "core"—your abdominal area—is especially important in riding. Various types of sit-ups and crunches can help you strengthen this region. Stretching exercises are also very helpful, especially in areas where you tend to be tight in the saddle (different riders battle with different personal areas of tension). To loosen and warm up your muscles, try to stretch for at least a few minutes before every ride.

The Turn-out Advantage

Studies show that young horses who are confined to stables have less bone-building activity than youngsters raised in large pastures. Daily exercise under saddle contributes to skeletal development in horses of all ages, but allowing a horse to play and wander around a field helps his bones grow even stronger. Regular turn-out (free time in a pasture) should, therefore, be an essential component of every horse's care.

body shape. Unfit horses' muscles are slacker-looking, softer to the touch, and seem to blend together. When they exercise, out-of-shape horses produce white, foamy sweat, whereas well-conditioned horses produce a clear sweat that gives them a sleek sheen.

The most accurate way to evaluate your horse's fitness is to measure his recovery time after a strenuous workout. (First learn how to estimate his baseline vital signs—see Chapter 21 for details.) Exercise him to the point where he starts to breathe heavily. Then stop, dismount, and time how long it takes his respiration and heart rate to come down. The faster they return to normal, the fitter he is. A well-conditioned athlete's heart rate and respiration may drop substantially in as little as three minutes after stopping work.

Dear Diary

Your next step is to write down a logical conditioning program for your horse. Try to plan for both the short term (about 30 days) and the long term (about 6 months). Map out your goals (competitions, trail rides, clinics, etc.) on a calendar and then count back weeks to plan what you need to do to prepare for them. The less fit your horse is and the higher-level your goals are, the longer your program needs to be. Use the principles explained below to plan a progressive, successful conditioning program.

While you're at your desk, dig up a fresh notebook to use as a training diary. Each time you ride, jot down a few notes about what you did and how your horse performed, including comments on his attitude, energy level, and recovery-time statistics. These notes will be very helpful to look back over as his training progresses.

Break Down to Build Up

Your horse's performance relies on his skeletal system, his cardiovascular system (lungs and heart), and his soft tissues (muscles, tendons, etc.). For all three systems, improvements in performance result from a repeated cycle of breakdown and repair. Incremental increases in workload stress the body, causing microdamage (tiny strains) to the tissues. During a subsequent rest period (24 to 48 hours after a hard workout), the body rebuilds itself, repairing the damaged tissue, making it stronger than it was before. If the process is rushed—workload is increased too rapidly or rest periods are too short—the microdamage can turn into serious damage.

The best conditioning programs use a rotating schedule that changes from day to day, allowing this breakdown/build-up process to work. Every strenuous workout, for example, should be followed by a day or two of easier rides.

To get your horse really fit, you'll need to ride him five to six days a week. However, you can help him maintain a moderate fitness level with just three to four rides per week. Try to spread his

Your horse will need a conditioning program for the kind of work you want to do together. Work with a professional to set and achieve your goals.

Barnwork—mucking stalls, carrying buckets, etc.—can also improve your fitness level. Try to be ambidextrous in everything you do (switching your hands on the pitchfork, carrying buckets of equal weight in each hand, etc.), so you strengthen both sides of your body equally.

Intensity vs. Distance

A good conditioning program "ups the ante"—raises the workload level—about once a week. When you do this, increase either the intensity or the distance (duration), but never increase both at the same time. So, for example, if you're training for endurance riding, add more fast work (trots and canters) one week, then extend the duration of your rides the following week.

Diversifying the activities you do will help keep your horse in better shape physically and mentally.

rest days evenly through the week, rather than clustering them in several days in a row. Also try to vary the exercise demands from day to day (never doing strenuous workouts two days in a row). Intersperse rest days and easier days among the harder days to give his body time to recover and rebuild.

Different types of workouts will develop a horse's body for different skills. For example, a horse conditioned with many slow trail rides will be better prepared for endurance races than for sports that require more explosive spurts of energy. Work with your trainer to devise a program that will mold your horse's skeletal, cardiovascular, and soft-tissue systems to suit the job you want him to do.

LSD (Long, Slow Distance)

The foundation of your basic-fitness program is long, slow distance. If your horse is really out of shape (just

coming back from a winter off or recovering from an injury), start walking him under saddle four to six days a week for three to four weeks. Increase the duration of each ride from about 20 minutes to about 1½ hours. At first, work on level, forgiving footing (good turf, sand, soft dirt roads, etc.). Gradually incorporate changes in terrain, such as rolling hills and steeper slopes. Avoid working on hard or rocky footing.

The next step is to add brief trots (up to 10 minutes) to your conditioning rides and begin easy schooling sessions in the arena. After another three weeks at this level, you're ready to add slow canters. Then, if you're planning on doing high-intensity activities, such as jumping, roping, and barrel racing, gradually begin working on those skills every few days.

Warm Up, Cool Down

Just like any other athlete, to avoid injuries, a horse should have a proper warm-up before each ride and a cool-down period afterward. For most types of exercise, a brisk ten-minute walk is usually adequate. In warm-up, this helps get the blood flowing and the muscles warm and ready for work; during the cool-down, it helps remove the lactic acid (a by-product of muscle exertion) from the muscles and initiates the repair-and-rebuild process.

Warming Up Together

Ask your instructor to give you a few stretching exercises to use to loosen up your own body in the saddle while your horse is warming up. To be safe, only do them in an enclosed arena at the walk, and always keep at least one hand on the reins.

Stronger in the Saddle

A good instructor will have plenty of exercises for strengthening and improving your position and balance in the saddle. Here are two time-proven techniques:

Riding without stirrups – Either take your stirrups off your saddle or cross them over your horse's withers in front of the saddle. Practice keeping your balance at the walk first before trying a trot. As your riding improves, you should be able to canter and even jump without stirrups.

Riding in "two point" – Instead of sitting in the saddle, stand up in your stirrups, balancing on your knees (your "two points"), keeping your lower legs still against your horse's sides, and dropping your weight down into your heels. Do this as long as you can at the walk. As your skills improve, try doing this at the trot and canter, over poles, and up and down hills.

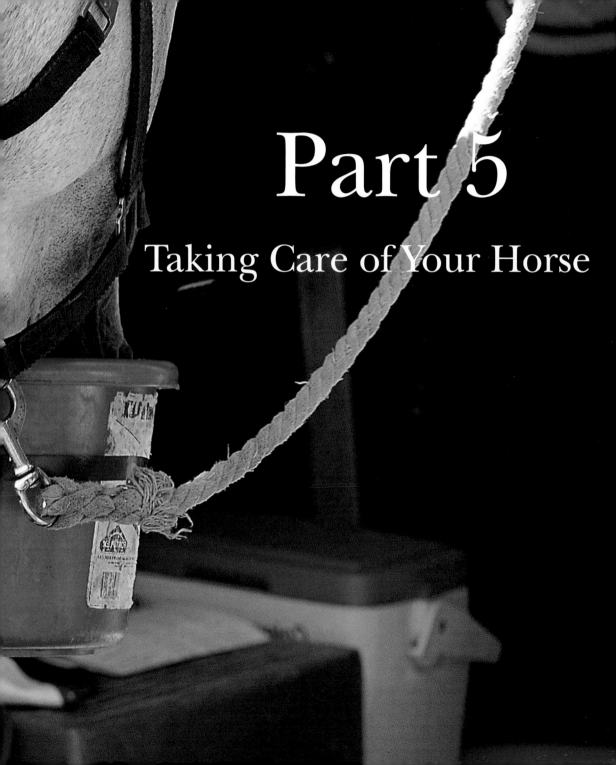

Part 5

Taking Care of Your Horse

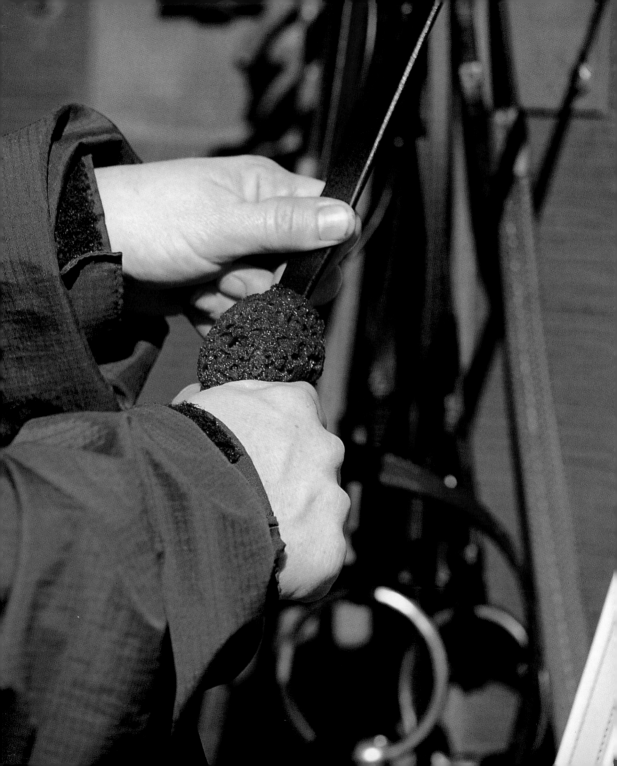

Chapter 17

The Daily Routine

Caring for a horse can be a lot like caring for a baby. You're entirely responsible for providing balanced, nutritious meals; keeping him clean and healthy; and protecting him from things that can hurt him—and things with which he can hurt himself. This chapter will focus on the daily care he'll need. (Feeding and nutrition are covered in Chapter 18.)

Fresh Water at All Times

Dehydration is a common contributor to equine health problems. To avoid it, give your horse access to clean, fresh water at all times. Monitor how much he normally drinks in a day, so you'll notice any changes. A significant drop in his thirst might indicate an ailment or a problem with the water (contaminants, etc.). A dramatic increase in his thirst not connected to increased exercise or hot weather may also indicate a health concern.

In the wintertime, check the water temperature often. Some horses won't drink as much if the water is near freezing. Insulated buckets and stock tank de-icers are available in many horse catalogs and farm-supply stores. Heated, automatic waterers are great timesavers, but be sure to buy one with a meter so you can continue to monitor your horse's water intake. Also be sure to install the waterer in a way that minimizes any chance of electrical hazards or failures.

Natural sources of water, such as streams and ponds, may not be reliable and may even be unsafe (for example, if the water becomes stagnant or contaminated from upstream sources). If your pasture contains a natural water source, provide a stock tank of clean water as well.

Clean, Dry Stall

It may sound like a thankless job, but mucking stalls is one of the most valuable services you can provide your horse. The moisture and ammonia fumes of his own manure and urine can contribute to respiratory, hoof, and skin ailments. The filth also attracts pesky insects. So, it's important to keep his stall as clean and dry as possible.

Don't rely on snow to provide your horse's water needs. Horses will eat snow to get some moisture, but they still need a clean source of fresh water.

Depending on how much time he spends in the stall (obviously, the more time he's turned out to pasture, the cleaner his stall will be), you'll need to clean it anywhere from one to three times a day. If possible, clean it while he's in the pasture or tied in the aisle. That way, he won't be exposed to the strong ammonia fumes you'll release while shifting the bedding (the straw, shavings, or other absorbent, cushioning material lining his stall floor)—and he won't be slowing down your progress by standing in your way.

Here's the basic routine:

★ With a manure fork, pick out the manure piles, trying not to remove too much clean bedding with them, and toss them into a wheelbarrow or muck bucket.

★ Scoop out all obvious wet or soiled bedding.

★ Shift the bedding around the stall to look for less obvious piles and wet spots.

★ If the stall floor is very damp and your horse will be away from it for several hours, push the bedding to the sides and allow the floor to air dry. (You can also sprinkle a little lime or stall freshener—available at feed and farm-supply stores—on the damp spots.)

★ Spread the bedding back across the stall evenly and add extra bedding as needed. A good general rule of thumb is two feet deep for straw bedding and one foot deep for shavings or sawdust. "Bank" the bedding on the edges: Pile it higher against the walls than in the center. This helps keep your horse from getting cast (rolling too close to the wall and not being able to push away from it with his legs to stand up).

One thorough daily cleaning is usually adequate. Picking out the obvious piles once or twice later in the day will make the next cleaning easier and keep your horse from getting too soiled when he lies down.

Manure Management

Once you've cleaned your horse's stall, where do you

Goldfish in the Water Trough?

You bet! Goldfish and some other species of fish, such as *Gambusia* fish (a kind of minnow, also known as mosquitofish), thrive well in large water troughs. They don't interfere with the horses, but they do feed aggressively on mosquito larvae, thus lowering the population of the bugs that transmit deadly diseases such as West Nile virus.

Horses need a steady supply of fresh, cool water. If you're traveling or competing with your horse, be sure to bring a bucket you can use to provide it for him.

put all of the soiled bedding and manure? You have a few options:

★ Spread it directly onto your fields with a manure spreader—a wagon-like contraption that flings manure out as you pull it with a tractor or other vehicle. Ideally, manure should be spread on pastures that won't be used for grazing horses or should be composted before spreading. Look for a manure spreader at a farm-supply store or in the newspaper classifieds. Store it far enough away from the barn to avoid attracting flies to the area, but still close enough to haul manure to it daily.

★ Give it away to gardeners. Advertise in your local paper, at garden-supply stores, or just put a "Free Manure" sign by your mailbox. Some farmers may even pay for your manure if it's the right composition for their particular crops.

Horse manure can be composted and spread on fields to provide fertilizer.

Live by the Rules

If you're boarding your horse, learn the barn rules and follow them!

If you keep him at home, create your own list of barn rules. Here are some good ones to include:

★ Minimize clutter in and around the barn. Remove anything a horse might bump into by mistake— tack trunks, saddle racks, etc.,—from the barn aisle and entrances.

★ Secure all doors and half-doors either open or closed, rather than allowing them to swing in the aisle where a horse might bang into them.

★ Keep all drains clear so floors don't flood and become dangerously slippery. Also keep a muck bucket and shovel handy to scoop up slippery manure piles from the aisle, wash stall, and grooming stall.

★ Make minor repairs around the barn immediately and put major repairs on the top of your "To Do" list. Putting these things off is asking for trouble!

★ Keep all horses a safe distance away from each other. No matter how tempting it is to let them meet, restrict their interactions to the turn-out pasture. Any encounter between horses, even friendly ones, can result in bites, kicks, or strikes reaching unintended targets (i.e., humans). When you lead your horse past another horse's stall, a horse in a paddock, or a tied-up horse, always give him a wide berth.

★ Keep your face a safe distance from your horse's face. Instead of kissing him on the nose, give him a good scratch on the withers. Even the nicest horses occasionally bite or nibble—and your horse doesn't know that your nose is more fragile than his. He'd prefer the scratch anyway.

★ Closely supervise any small children, dogs, or other unpredictable, noisy creatures. If a child wants to pat your horse, lift him up to pat his neck, keeping him clear of hooves and teeth.

★ Compost it. Manure and soiled bedding make an excellent fertilizer if they've been properly composted for a few months. The composting process kills parasites and reduces the size of the pile significantly. Ask a gardening expert how to construct and maintain a good compost heap.

★ Hire a waste-management company to remove it weekly, via a heavy duty-dumpster.

Barn Safety

Unfortunately, because of horses' flighty nature and tremendous size, injuries are common around barns. To keep accidents to a minimum, try to think like a horse. Learn to predict what might spook him—a car door slamming, loud yells, the gurgle of a hose when you turn the water on, etc. Keep a

Be aware of what might startle your horse around the barn, including debris falling from the hay loft.

few feet of space between you and him when you think he might move suddenly in reaction to such things.

To avoid spooking him yourself, maintain a calm, quiet demeanor, making all of your motions predictable and deliberate (i.e., no dramatic arm-swinging, shouting, or sneaking up on him from behind). Even if other events of the day involving your work, family, etc., have preoccupied your thoughts, when you enter the barn, focus on the horse and pay close attention to things going on around you.

Prevent Barn Fires

Far too many horses are killed in barn fires every year, many of which could be prevented. Most barn fires result from electrical malfunctions, human error, or mere carelessness. The following are just some of the preventative measures every barn owner should take. Ask your insurance agent and/or local fire department to suggest more.

★ Prohibit smoking in or around the barn.

★ Regularly sweep cobwebs from the walls and light fixtures. Keep all other flammable clutter to a minimum.

★ Have a licensed electrician update your electrical system. Replace all old or frayed wires; run wiring through protective conduits; place outlets well out of horses' reach; and check that your system provides enough power for the appliances, lights, fans, etc., you use in the barn.

★ If possible, store hay, bedding, and other combustibles in a building separate from the barn.

★ Park and store all gas-powered vehicles, appliances, and flammable materials (pesticides, cleaning fluids, etc.) away from the barn.

★ Install smoke alarms, fire extinguishers, well-grounded lightning rods, and, if you can afford one, a sprinkler system.

★ Hang a halter and lead rope next to each horse's stall so you can lead him out quickly in an emergency.

★ Post your address and directions to the barn next to the telephone so

Use a clean, dry saddle pad every time you ride, no matter the season.

whoever calls the fire department (or any other emergency service) can read them over the phone.

Avoid Blanket Boo-boos

If you use blankets on your horse, you'll want to remember the following: Do not throw a blanket up over your horse's back. His natural reaction may be to jump away, or even to kick out at it. The blanket buckles may also smack the wall on the other side, making him or another horse spook at the noise, and/or possibly shattering windows and light bulbs. Instead, fold the blanket a few times and slowly raise it to his withers before slowly unfolding it over his body.

Also, always attach the chest buckle first when putting a blanket on and detach it last when taking it off. This avoids the unfortunately common, and often disastrous, situation of a blanket shifting backward and belly or leg straps pinching or tickling the horse in the flank area, which may set off a kicking or bucking reaction.

Put your horse's halter and lead rope on before adjusting his blankets. This way you can prevent him from turning away from you and possibly kicking out at you—or simply taking off half-dressed.

Store the blankets safely: Instead of hanging your horse's blankets on hooks in the aisle, on which he can catch a halter or injure himself, install a smooth, horizontal bar, with rounded edges (preferably one that folds flat against the wall when not in use) at about chest height on the stall door or aisle wall. Never install a blanket bar where a horse can reach it from his stall. Many horses have broken their jawbones by getting their lower jaws caught underneath blanket bars.

Finally, check your horse's coat underneath the blanket daily. Look for rubbed spots, sores, and sweat (from overheating).

Nose-to-Toes, Ears-to-Tail Check

No matter how hurried you are on any given day, always take a second to give your horse a "once-over" inspection. Start at his head and work your way down one side, briefly scanning every part of his body as you go, then walk around to the other side and do the same there. Look for anything out of the ordinary: cuts, scrapes, swellings, missing shoes. Pay close attention to the look in his eye (bright or dull? anxious or uninterested?), the way he's carrying his head (up and alert or low and depressed?), and the way he's standing on his feet.

Often, a horse will rest one hind leg, cocking it backward and shifting the weight to the other leg temporarily. This is normal. However, if your horse is clearly uncomfortable putting weight on one leg, look more closely for any obvious source of discomfort, then call the veterinarian. (In later chapters, I'll tell you what to do if you do detect something out of the ordinary.)

Daily Turn-Out

Ideally, your horse should be turned out in a paddock or pasture for at least several hours each day. In hot, humid weather, turn him out at night or during the cooler hours of the day. Try not to turn him out in extremely cold, windy weather unless he has access to some sort of shelter or windbreak.

Before you turn him out, always check that the fencing is intact and in good repair. Also check that the footing is safe. Icy and extremely muddy footing can be dangerously slippery, particularly if your horse's shoes aren't equipped with extra traction. Snow, on the other hand, usually makes a relatively safe surface for horses—although it can ball up in their shoes, interfering with their balance and movement.

Always lead your horse to and from the pasture with a halter and lead rope. When you enter and exit the pasture, be sure that other horses aren't near enough to sneak through the gate or trap you in a scuffle. Swing the gate widely enough so that your horse won't risk bumping a shoulder

Runner or Keeper?

Bridle straps are held in place by two different features: runners, which are loops that move up and down the strap; and keepers, the loops that are stitched into the strap, next to the buckles.
When adjusting your bridle, pull each strap through its keeper first, then secure the end in place with its runner.

Keeping your tack clean by washing the sweat and grime off it after every use will lengthen its life significantly.

203

or hip as he passes through. Before releasing him, turn him to face the gate and ask him to stand still. (Many people incur injuries when horses race past them through pasture gates or wheel and kick out with enthusiasm when they're set free.)

You might think that jockeys are short people who race each other on fast horses. The word "jockey," however, is also used to describe black, greasy lumps of dirt that accumulate on infrequently cleaned tack. To remove these jockeys, try scraping them with your fingernail or scrubbing them off with a toothbrush. Then get your tack on a more regular cleaning schedule!

Tack Care

The better you treat your tack (saddle, bridle, etc.), the longer it will last and the more comfortable your horse will be. Clean, polished tack also makes a much better impression on a horse-show judge than dull, grimy tack. Most importantly, well-maintained tack is less likely to break suddenly while you're balanced precariously over your moving horse. Regular inspections for cracks, loose stitching, stretched holes, and leather that's worn thin might one day save you a trip to the emergency room.

The best way to maintain tack is by wiping it with a damp cloth after every ride, then giving it a thorough cleaning about once a week. Dust, mud, and salt (from sweat) will work their way into the grain of the leather, weakening its internal structure. Where you store your tack is crucial, too. Keep it in the driest, cleanest place you can, out of direct sunlight. Mold will develop on tack left in a damp place; dramatic changes in temperature will draw the moisture out of leather; and rodents, cats, horses, and other beasties may scratch and chew on tack left within their reach.

Tack-Cleaning Tips
Leather Tack

★ Disassemble all parts of your bridle and saddle. (This is the tricky part—pay close attention as you go so you'll remember how to put them back together again when you're done.)

★ Wash the stirrups and bit with warm water and soap, scrubbing any grime off with a toothbrush. Then polish all of the metal on your tack (except for the part of the bit that actually goes in your horse's mouth) with regular metal polish, trying not to get the polish on any leather.

★ With a damp cloth or sponge, apply a cleaning soap to the leather in a circular motion. Use a gentle soap such as castile soap or an oil-based product made specifically for cleaning leather. (Don't use glycerine soap at this stage. It actually seals the pores of the leather, prohibiting the conditioner—in your next step—from soaking in.) Rinse the sponge and wipe off any soap residue.

★ If the leather looks at all dry or brittle, lightly coat it with a conditioner. You can use a leather conditioner sold through tack stores and catalogs or try pure neatsfoot oil, plain olive oil, or vegetable oil. Avoid mineral oils or baby oil, which can damage leather. Also avoid over-oiling: making leather too soft and supple can weaken it, too.

★ Finally, to make your leather water-resistant and give it an extra shine, wet a bar of glycerine soap and apply it directly—or use a damp cloth or sponge to wipe it on.

Synthetic Tack

Synthetic tack is much simpler to care for: Simply wash with water and mild soap (dishwashing liquid or a cleaning product made specifically for synthetic tack—no glycerine soap), then allow it to air-dry.

Suede

If your tack contains any suede (for example, cushioning on your saddle's knee roll), be careful to keep saddle soaps, oils, conditioners, and metal polish clear of it. To make suede look new again, gently brush it with a fingernail brush.

Saddle Pads

The best way to keep your horse's skin and coat underneath the saddle healthy is to use a clean, dry saddle pad every time you ride. Always thoroughly air-dry sweaty saddle pads and throw them in the washer as soon as they start to accumulate dirt and dried sweat. (This goes for any washable materials you use on your horse.)

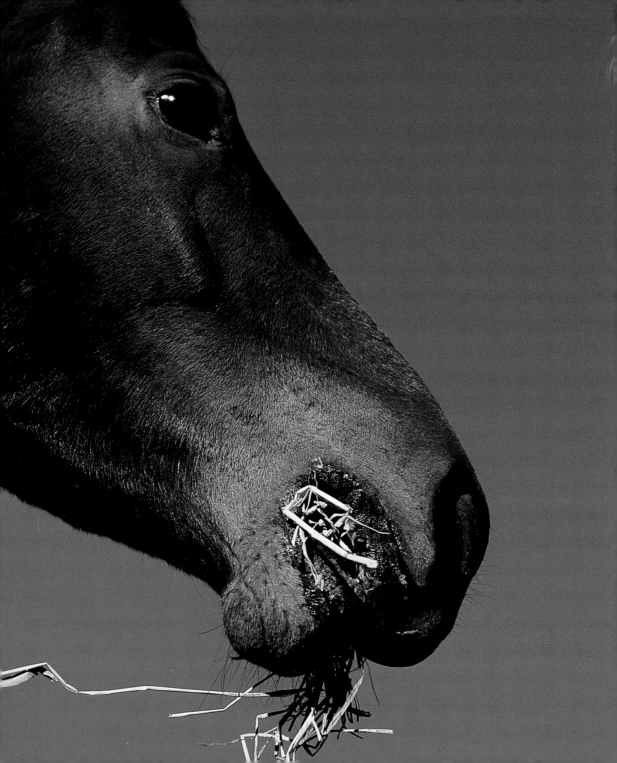

Chapter 18

Feeding and Nutrition

Overall health starts from the inside out, and because you determine what goes into your horse, you play a big part in keeping him as healthy as possible. By feeding him a diet naturally suited to his system, you can minimize digestive upsets and more serious gastrointestinal problems. His lustrous coat, proper energy level, clear eyes and nose, and overall appetite for life will be your reward for taking the best care of him you can.

Feed Small, Frequent Meals

This should be the number-one rule in all feeding programs. Horses have very small stomachs relative to their body size. When you overload your horse's stomach with a large grain meal—greater than 6 to 7 pounds—much of the food is pushed through the small intestine undigested. High-starch (high-carbohydrate) foods, such as oats, corn, and other grains, then start to ferment in the hindgut (the large intestine and cecum), disrupting the normal microbial population there, which then can lead to colic (gastrointestinal distress that can cause severe pain and even death) or diarrhea. Horses are better at digesting roughage, such as hay and grass. These high-fiber, low-starch foods move more slowly through the digestive system, causing less trouble.

Long periods between meals are equally unhealthy. Unlike humans, horses produce digestive acids in their stomachs 24 hours a day. So, if there's no food in your horse's stomach for a long period of time, the acids may start irritating his stomach lining, causing ulcers. Studies show that about 60 percent of show horses suffer from ulcers.

The healthiest way to feed your horse is to try to mimic his natural grazing state. Give him as much access to green pasture as you can and, when he's stabled, provide him with a constant supply of good-quality hay. Don't wait for him to clean up his hay before giving him more. This way, he won't become anxious about when his next meal's showing up—and he'll learn to relax and snack slowly throughout the day. (If he's a real glutton and grows overweight on this feeding program, cut down on the caloric content of his diet. More on that later.)

A simple diet of good pasture and/or high-quality hay can provide most average horses in moderate work with all of the calories and nutrients they need. To maintain a good weight, some horses may require additional calories, usually provided in the form of grain. (To evaluate your horse's weight, see below.)

Few horses need more than 4 to 8 pounds of grain per day. If you do

feed your horse grain, try to spread his meals out throughout the day. Avoid feeding a single grain meal of more than 6 to 7 pounds.

Mimicking a horse's natural grazing state by allowing him plenty of time in grassy pastures is the first step in proper nutrition.

Skinny, Fat, or Just Right?

When evaluating your horse's feeding program, the first thing you need to judge is his body condition. To decide if he's too fat, too thin, or just right, look closely at and run your hand over his neck, withers, shoulders, ribs, back, loins, rump, and tailhead (the area around the top of his tail). These areas should be nicely rounded by muscle, but not covered with extra fatty bulges. You should be able to feel, but not see, your horse's ribs. You should not be able to feel the individual vertebrae in his neck or tailhead. Nor should you see the bony ends of the vertebrae in his back and loins sticking up, creating a bony topline.

When evaluating your horse, take several things into consideration. If he's a "light breed," like an Arabian, Thoroughbred, or Morgan, he should look leaner than a naturally heavier-built warmblood, American Quarter Horse, or draft horse. Ideal condition varies somewhat from discipline to discipline, too. For example, a show hunter or western pleasure horse is expected to look rounder and fleshier than an endurance horse or eventer.

It's important to monitor your horse's body condition closely, particularly during winter. Long winter coats and blankets can hide major weight changes. A thin, ribby horse may appear deceptively fat underneath his thick winter coat. Run your hands over your horse's body regularly to evaluate his true condition—your regular grooming sessions are great opportunities for this.

Hay is dried grass compacted into bales, which are held together by string or wire that needs to be cut before being fed to horses. the bales when opened, break into individual flakes.

Counting Calories

To help your horse gain or lose weight, you need to count calories. Because the same-sized coffee can of grain or flake of hay might have a completely different caloric content depending on the type of grain or hay you're feeding, it's very important to quantify your horse's diet with standard weight and calorie measurements.

You'll need a scale (bathroom type scales work well) and calorie-per-pound estimates of your horse's grain and hay. By weighing his daily ration, then multiplying that weight by the calorie-per-pound ratio, you can estimate his daily caloric intake. (For sample calorie-per-pound ratios and help calculating your horse's caloric intake, see the box, "Comparing Calories.")

If your horse needs to gain weight, simply substitute some of his current diet with a more calorie-dense foodstuff. (I'll recommend some higher-calorie foods later on.) If he needs to lose weight, cut down his calories by feeding him lower-calorie hay and less grain—or cut the grain out altogether.

Horses have sensitive digestive systems, so make any diet increases very gradually. Introduce new grain or hay

Different foods have different nutritive values. These need to be understood and assessed relative to your particular horse to keep him at his best weight and energy level.

Comparing Calories

To calculate your horse's daily caloric intake, weigh each portion of his diet and use the following multiplying factors to convert the weights to calories. For example, if he eats 8 pounds of "high fat" commercial concentrate and 10 pounds of full-bloom alfalfa hay each day, that's: 8 pounds x 1,500 calories/pound = 12,000 calories, plus 10 pounds x 1,000 calories/pound = 10,000 calories = a total diet of 22,000 calories per day. Once you've decided how much weight he needs to gain or lose, use this chart to decide how to change his diet to increase or decrease calories.

Conversion Ratios: Food Sources in Calories per Pound

Early-bloom Alfalfa Hay:	1,100
Full-bloom Alfalfa Hay:	1,000
Early-bloom Grass Hay*:	800 to 900
Full-bloom Grass Hay:	700 to 800
Alfalfa pellets:	1,100
Beet pulp:	1,100
Commercial concentrate (less than 6 percent fat):	1,400 to 1,450
Commercial concentrate (6 to 8 percent fat):	1,500 to 1,600
Barley:	1,650
Corn:	1,700
Oats:	1,200
Rice bran:	1,300
Wheat bran:	1,200
Soybean meal:	1,600
Vegetable oil (one measuring cup):	1,600

*Includes timothy, bromegrass, and Bermuda grass hays.

Source: National Research Council. *Nutrient Requirements of Horses,* 1989.

Do you know how your mother always told you to wait 30 minutes after lunch before swimming, so you didn't get a cramp and drown? Well, horses can have similar tummy trouble if you ride them hard too soon after a big meal. So, allow at least 30 minutes after a small grain meal (one or two pounds of grain) and two to three hours after a large meal (three or more pounds of grain) before exercising your horse.

Hay is usually safe to feed before exercise, because it doesn't trigger the same blood-sugar drop that grains do. Feeding a steady supply of hay during hot weather actually helps your horse replace fluids lost in sweat, because he'll drink approximately two pounds of water for every pound of hay he eats.

in very small amounts (about a pound a day).

Protein Requirements

Most people feed their horses a combination of commercial grain and hay. One of the things you want to look at on the label of your commercial grain is the protein content. Mature horses only need about 11 to 12 percent of their total diets (including hay and pasture) to be protein. Regular pasture and grass hays can be 10 percent protein or less, but alfalfa hay can be as much as 14 to 22 percent protein. So, if you're feeding an alfalfa or alfalfa-mix hay, balance it with a low-protein grain.

Roughage is #1

Roughage (hay, grass, and other high-fiber feed sources) is not only the healthiest, most natural feed for horses, it's also a great way to keep your horse busy. Eating roughage simply takes up more time than eating concentrated grains. The less time your horse spends eating, the more bored he'll become and the more likely he'll be to develop bad habits such as chewing on the fences.

Experts recommend feeding a horse enough daily roughage to equal 1.5 percent or more of his body weight. For example, if your horse weighs 1,000 pounds, he should eat at least 15 pounds of hay per day. To estimate his weight, buy a "weight tape" (measuring tape that you wrap around your horse's girth) at your local tack or feed store.

Depending on your region, climate, and pasture-management routine, grass can make up a large percentage of your horse's daily roughage. Be prepared to compensate with other sources during slower growing seasons, on days when your horse can't be turned out, and on days when pastures are covered with snow. Roughage has the

There's a reason for the saying, "Hay is for horses." Hay provides many of a horse's essential dietary requirements.

added benefit of creating heat as it breaks down in your horse's gut. It can actually help keep him warm during cold spells. So, increase hay portions in the wintertime, especially if he has limited access to pasture.

Evaluating Hay Quality

Hay varies a great deal in quality depending on how, where, and when it's harvested. What might be good enough for a herd of cows may not be palatable—or even safe—for your horse. To find the right kind of hay, ask other local horse people or the staff at your local feed store to recommend a reputable hay farmer. Then ask the farmer to open a sample hay bale for you to inspect. Here's what to look for:

★ Fine-stemmed, green, leafy hay that's soft to the touch.

★ Hay harvested within a year of purchase (nutritional value in the hay declines if you feed it later than a year after it's been cut).

⋆ Hay harvested during early bloom (for legume hay like alfalfa and clover) or before seed heads have formed (in grass hay).

⋆ Avoid hay that smells or looks moldy, dusty, or fermented, or that is excessively sun-bleached (a little discoloration on the outside of bales is usually okay).

⋆ Avoid hay that contains significant amounts of dirt, debris, or weeds.

⋆ Look for signs of insect infestation or disease.

⋆ Don't buy bales that seem excessively heavy for their size. Also watch out for bales that are warm to the touch—they may contain excess moisture that could result in mold.

If you have any particular questions about the hay you're purchasing or if you want to determine its exact nutritional content (vitamins, minerals, moisture content, etc.), send a sample of it to your agricultural extension agent.

If your horse has respiratory problems or if your hay is slightly dusty, soak it in water for 20 minutes to an hour before mealtime. In hot, humid weather soak only as much as you think your horse will eat in four to six hours (one-third to one-half of his daily ration) to prevent mold or fermentation problems. Drain the hay thoroughly before feeding it in a manger, hay net, or on top of a rubber mat in the corner of his stall. Remove uneaten hay daily to prevent mold and fungus accumulation.

Salt

Salt is another crucial component in your horse's diet. Most commercial grains include some salt, but depending on how hot the weather is and how much your horse is working (i.e., how much salt he's losing in sweat), this may not be enough. Putting a salt block in his stall and pasture allows him to replenish whatever extra salt he's lost. You'll find salt blocks at your local feed stores—plain ones are white and mineral-supplemented ones are a reddish color.

A mineral block is usually preferable, except in cases where your horse is sweating a great deal and licking or biting the block constantly. This indicates that his salt needs are higher and you should give him only a white salt block so he doesn't take in too much of the other minerals for which he doesn't have an increased need.

To replace the minerals lost in sweat during heavy exercise periods, add them to your horse's grain or administer them to him via an oral paste syringe. Either buy a commercial electrolyte product from a catalog or feed store or use this homemade recipe: Mix one pound table salt, 12 ounces "lite" salt, and one to two ounces of calcium magnesium chloride (also known as dolomite, which can be found in tablets or powder form at grocery and health-food stores) with water and ¼ cup molasses. Give your horse one to two ounces of this mixture per hour of hard work. Do not feed it unless the horse has been sweating.

Supplements – Does He Really Need Them?

The equine nutritional supplement market is a booming business. There are herbal remedies, synthetic tonics, mineral blends, and other food additives advertised to enhance your horse's energy, coat shine, attitude, etc., and to cure ailments ranging from arthritis to anemia. Some of them seem to work; some don't.

The soil in some regions of the country may have deficiencies or excesses of particular minerals, which can influence the nutritional content of your horse's grain, hay, and pasture. For example, selenium, an essential nutrient in equine diets, tends to be low in areas with relatively high rainfall, such as parts of the Northeast, Southeast, Pacific Northwest, and upper Midwest. The Great Plains region, on the other hand, is naturally selenium-rich. Although selenium deficiencies are more common in horses, selenium toxicosis (overdose) can happen, too, so

> The best rule is: Keep it simple. If your horse exhibits signs of general good health—nice coat, bright eyes, and normal weight—he probably doesn't need any supplements.

Over-supplementing your horse's diet may be more dangerous than undersupplementing.

Horses can get competitive—and even aggressive—when fed in groups. If you can't separate your horses at feeding time, spread their feed pans or buckets far apart. (Stay on your toes! You don't want to get caught in between horses chasing each other away from buckets.) Even better, buy individual nose bags. These prevent horses who are fed different kinds or amounts of food from stealing from one another.

neither extreme is desirable.

Most commercial feeds contain added vitamins and minerals (including selenium). If you believe that something may be either lacking or present in unsafe amounts in your horse's diet, ask your veterinarian, agricultural extension agent, and/or local feed company representatives if they recommend particular feeds or vitamin or mineral supplements for horses in your area.

Before adding any supplement to your horse's diet, do as much research as you can on the quality and safety of its contents. Some of the ingredients in equine supplements, such as certain herbs, have not been extensively tested for safety and efficacy.

Even vitamin and mineral supplements can create imbalances in your horse's system if he ingests them at abnormally high levels. Overdoses of vitamins A and D, iodine, and selenium, for example, can be toxic. Even a safe dosage of one mineral supplement may interfere with the absorption of other minerals, leading to deficiencies. Be careful to read the labels on everything you feed (grain as well as supplements) to avoid oversupplementing a vitamin or mineral by mistake. Learn as much as you can about a product, and consult the experts, before trying it on your horse.

Fattening Up

Most horses like to eat. However, the occasional fussy eater or high-energy horse may need a little help keeping weight on. If your horse turns his nose up at a meal, try switching to a tastier sweet feed (a grain containing molasses) or mixing some molasses in with his grain. Also try breaking his daily grain ration into smaller, more frequent servings.

Right: Horses—like the rest of us—love treats, and healthy ones like carrots and apples are some of their favorites.

The best way to help a horse gain weight is to improve the quality and quantity of his roughage. If he gets a low-calorie timothy hay, for example, switch to a higher-calorie alfalfa mix. Or consider adding beet pulp, a high-fiber, low-starch roughage source, to his diet. Beet pulp swells when moistened, so always soak it thoroughly before giving it to your horse. You can safely feed as much as five or six pounds of beet pulp or beet-pulp pellets per day.

High-fat sources can also help a horse gain weight. You can safely increase your horse's fat intake to up to 10 percent of his diet. Feed companies offer a variety of "high-energy" grains and high-fat supplements, which contain anywhere from 6 to 22 percent fat (regular feeds contain less than 4 percent fat), but are still relatively low in starch.

Bran Mashes

One of the most popular "comfort foods" people have fed horses for generations is a wheat bran mash—a warm, watery slurry of wheat bran and other yummy treats, like grain, apples, and carrots. Wheat bran is made from the outer husk of grain. For years, it was erroneously believed to have a laxative effect. In truth, the water added to the bran simply increases water intake. Picky eaters seem to find it tastier than other feeds. A mash can also be useful as a base for mixing with less palatable things, such as electrolytes or medications. However, it is very high in phosphorus and should not be fed daily or in large amounts. To learn how to make a bran mash, ask your instructor or another local horse person for their recipe.

Junk Food for Horses?

Horses often enjoy eating some really odd things. The following is a list of nontraditional foods that veterinarians and horse owners around the world have reported horses consuming safely.

Acceptable treats (fed in limited quantities—less than 1 to 2 pounds per feeding):

★ Carrots, apples, grapes, bananas, peas, green beans, dried beans (such as pinto, red, fava—should be cooked or heat treated), watermelon rinds, squash, mangoes (not the seeds), raisins, bread/bagels/cake (not if they contain chocolate or poppy seeds), pasta, macaroni, potato chips and potato products, rice products (not raw rice), barley products, corn products, dairy products, eggs, fruit juices, lettuce, celery, most dog and cat foods, hot dogs, hamburgers, tuna fish, ham and even roastbeef sandwiches!

Okay in very small quantities (less than 2 to 4 ounces per day), but beware of feeding large quantities:

★ Garlic and onions (large amounts may cause anemia), brassica species (cabbage, broccoli, kale, chard, collard greens, brussel sprouts), sugar candies such as jelly beans, gummy bears, peppermints, etc., avocado (not the skin or seeds), sunflower seeds, rhubarb stems (not the leaves or roots), spinach, turnips, radishes.

Safe in very limited quantities but may cause positive drug tests, for instance, at competitions:

★ Chocolate in any form, poppy seeds, non-decaffeinated coffee or tea in any form, caffeinated sodas, tobacco, some dog/cat foods (beware of the ingredient, "bakery waste," which may contain chocolate), hot pepper/chili-flavored products (nacho chips, etc.), licorice, carrots (may cause positive drug test if fed in very large quantities—over five pounds/day), valerian root, persimmons (seeds also may cause impaction colic, a very serious condition), cinnamon products, nutmeg, yucca, sassafras.

A simpler, cheaper source of fat is vegetable oil. Horses like corn oil the best, but others, such as soybean, canola, and flaxseed oil, are also acceptable supplements. One cup of vegetable oil provides about the same amount of calories as one pound of grain.

When you introduce oil to your horse's meal, start with just a few tablespoons, then slowly increase the amount up to as much as two cups per day, if necessary.

Remember, whenever you make changes or additions to your horse's diet, make them very gradually. Any dramatic adjustment can disrupt his digestive system.

Feeding Treats

Most horses love treats: apples, carrots, "horse cookies," peppermints, etc. Unfortunately, horses fed lots of treats often get pushy and develop bad habits like nipping and biting. If you feed your horse treats, try to use them as a teaching tool. Ask him to do a task first—pick up a hoof or lower his head—then praise him and give him the treat. If you make this very clear, he'll learn to associate the task with the praise and the treat—and won't "beg" for treats in other situations. Another way to feed treats without encouraging bad habits is to toss them into your horse's grain bucket.

Whenever feeding a treat by hand, always be very careful to hold it in the middle of your palm, with your fingers stretched out flat. It's easy for a horse to mistake fingers for carrots, so keep them clear of his teeth!

Chapter 19

Bug Patrol

Horses' arch enemies are flies, mosquitoes, and other pesky insects. On the worst summer and fall days, these tiny beasts can harass and torment your four-legged friend into a running, head-shaking, foot-stomping, tail-swishing frenzy. In very buggy regions, insects are a leading cause of weight loss, shoe loss (from foot stomping), and distracted behavior under saddle. They're also transmitters of many diseases.

*C*hemical companies have waged a losing war against bugs for decades. Each new generation of products they come up with is safer, and more environmentally friendly, but the bugs always seem to be one step ahead of them. The ingredients most commonly found in today's fly-control products are "pyrethroids," a family of synthetic chemicals related to a natural ingredient of certain chrysanthemums. They're safe and effective but, like any other insecticides, vulnerable to growing resistance in bug populations.

Fighting Enemy #1, Mosquitoes

One of the biggest threats facing horses today is West Nile virus, a highly fatal mosquito-borne disease. Although they are not mentioned in the press as frequently, several other mosquito-borne encephalitis diseases kill horses every year as well. Vaccines are available—and highly recommended—but they're not 100 percent effective, so mosquito control is still an important line of defense.

The best way to keep mosquitoes in check is to eliminate their breeding sites:

- Remove standing water from all containers (potted plants, tires, tarps, recycling bins with bottle caps and cans, etc.).
- Clean rain gutters in early spring and keep them clear throughout the year.
- Change water in birdbaths and water troughs twice a week.
- Drain or fill puddles that linger for more than a few days.
- Add mosquitofish (also known as *Gambusia*) to ornamental ponds, water troughs, ditches, and other standing water that can't be drained. (First ask your county pest control agent if it's legal to introduce these minnows in your local ecosystem.)

Cleaner Barns = Fewer Bugs

Good barn management is your best defense against "filth flies"—the flies that breed in manure, spilled feed, bedding, decaying vegetation, and other moist, warm, organic matter. In the barnyard area, horses are most plagued by house flies (which don't bite, but do annoy animals by feeding on moisture on their muzzles, eyes, and open wounds) and stable flies (which tend to attack the legs with very painful bites, causing horses to stamp their feet violently).

In just a few generations, insects can evolve to resist a particular chemical. The more heavily we use an insecticide, the faster the bugs develop resistance to it. Experts recommend saving insecticides for extremely buggy times and otherwise relying more on chemical-free solutions.

Fighting Flies

To fight filth flies, try to minimize places where they can breed:

- ★ Remove manure and soiled bedding from stalls daily.
- ★ Locate the manure pile far away from the barn and remove it regularly (daily, if possible, during the summertime).
- ★ If you spread manure on your fields, do it on the ones farthest from the barn. If possible, spread it on ones where horses won't be grazed.
- ★ Use shavings or sawdust instead of straw for bedding (flies prefer straw).
- ★ Keep the barn well ventilated, encouraging good airflow, which dries manure faster.

A barn that's kept as clean as possible goes a long way toward discouraging bugs and other pesty critters.

Good Horsekeeping

 ★ Thoroughly clean and air out unoccupied stalls.
 ★ Store all feed and supplements in airtight containers.
 ★ Remove uneaten grain from horses' stalls immediately after meals, and clear out accumulated uneaten hay weekly. (If you soak your horse's hay, remove uneaten portions daily.)
 ★ Scrub water buckets and feed tubs at least weekly.
 ★ Throw all garbage in trashcans with secure lids and empty cans weekly.
 ★ Keep human eating areas clean.
 ★ Sweep barn aisles, ledges, etc., regularly.
 ★ Keep your horse and all of his tack and equipment as clean as possible. (Sweat, dirt, and manure stains attract bugs.) Rinse the saliva, grass, etc., off of his bit when you take off his bridle. Rinse muddy boots as soon as he comes in from a ride or from the pasture. If you have a washing machine and dryer, wash blankets and saddle pads frequently.

Fighting Other Insects

Pasture bugs are harder to combat because they breed in sites you have less control over, such as cattle manure, marshy areas, streams, and ponds. Even if you maintain your own property well, bugs can travel from several miles away to feed on your horses. Common pasture pests include horse flies, deer flies, face flies, horn flies, black flies, biting midges (no-see-ums), and mosquitoes.

Here are some things you can do to try to minimize their populations:

 ★ Scrub, rinse, and refill water troughs in paddocks at least once a week (twice a week during mosquito season).
 ★ Don't mow grass when it's wet. Spread grass clippings from lawns and pastures out so they dry well (or compost them).
 ★ Turn your horse out to pasture when the bugs are less active. In mosquito season, for example, avoid turning your horse out at dusk and dawn, when many mosquito species feed.
 ★ Keep areas around run-in sheds clean and dry.

Chemical-Free Solutions

If you plan ahead, you can get a jump on bug populations before the season begins. Here are some popular, effective control methods:

Bug Eaters

Several commercial companies sell "beneficial insects" that eat pest insects. These tiny fly parasitoids, or "parasitic wasps," target house and stable flies and, to a lesser extent, horn flies, by feeding on flies in their developing stages. These wasps have stingers, but they never use them on humans or other animals.

To build up an effective parasitoid population on your property, start your program three to four weeks before the normal fly season begins; continue releasing wasps every two to four weeks until first frost. A good general rule of thumb is to release about 1,000 parasitized fly pupae (the life stage in which companies deliver parasitic wasps) per horse. Experts recommend requesting the *Muscidifurax raptor* species, currently the most effective against insect pests on horse farms. Ask your distributor for more specific instructions on how to time and locate your parasitoid releases.

To protect horses against West Nile Virus and other mosquito-borne diseases, avoid turning them out at dusk or dawn.

Bug Baits and Traps

Several fly-control products on the market attract bugs using the bugs' own chemical attractants (fly pheromones). Some "baits" are combined with insecticides, but many simply use insecticide-free attractants to catch the flies in traps or on sticky surfaces. These are safe to use in and around the barn, even in the presence of fly parasitoids.

In the pasture, several innovative traps are proving effective against pests. Olson Products' simple, nontoxic Biting Fly Trap® reflects light in the ultraviolet range, which is particularly attractive to stable flies. It can trap thousands of flies in just a few days. The Epps Biting Fly Trap® uses a different design to mimic an animal standing in the field. Its dark panels on leg-like supports attract horse flies, deer flies, and stable flies, then catch them with a clear pane of plastic film above a tray of soapy water.

The best traps for catching mosquitoes, no-see-ums, and some other biting insects are devices that emit carbon

Build a Bat House

Encouraging bats to take up residence on your property is a great way to cut down on your bug population. Ninety percent of bats eat insects; those that do feed mostly at night and make mosquitoes about 10 percent of their diet. They won't cure a mosquito problem, but they'll certainly help. Furthermore, they're very safe to have around people and horses. The only danger they may pose is as transmitters of rabies. However, bat-to-horse rabies transmission is very rare and bat-to-human transmission usually only happens when a human picks a diseased bat up off of the ground.

On the other hand, bats may be sensitive to insecticides, so be sure your bug-control program isn't hazardous to their health. To purchase a bat house or learn how to make one yourself, go to www.batcon.org. Some bat colonies stay year-round, spending the winter in a modified hibernation state. Others migrate to large caves as winter approaches. The added bonus: bat guano (droppings) is one of the best organic fertilizers there is—great for your garden!

dioxide. Most also use octenol, a mosquito attractant. Another effective trap, The Sonic Web™ Biting Insect Control emits the sound of a dog's heartbeat to attract blood-seeking insects.

One fly-control product that experts no longer recommend is the "zapper," which uses black light to attract flying insects and then kills them with an electric current. Not only do these devices kill beneficial insects, they also burn the bugs so thoroughly that their harmful bacteria are released into the air. New, safer black-light products use sticky boards, rather than electric zappers, to catch bugs.

If you do purchase a trap, position it out of your horse's reach. Set it up just outside the pasture or, if you locate it within the field, build a fence around the trap to protect it from curious noses and hooves.

The Old Reliable: Sticky Tape

One of the tried-and-true bug killers in barns and run-in sheds is double-sided "sticky tape." It's cheap, insecticide-free, and now available in a variety of forms, ranging from traditional vertically hanging strips to large, banner-like reel-to-reel systems that can be rolled to expose new tape as the old is used up.

Fly-Free Clothing

Want to fight flies with style? Buy your horse a crocheted fly "bonnet" (available in various colors). Fitted over his ears and under his halter or bridle, a bonnet dangles just above his eyes, sweeping away bothersome gnats and face flies—and often eliminating annoying head shaking during your rides. To protect his eyes from pesky face flies, buy a mesh face mask with fuzzy fleece edges. Fit the mask carefully to his face, being sure it's not pressing on his eyes, and that it is snug enough to prevent shifting and allowing bugs to sneak in under the edges.

A wide variety of other fly "clothing" is available through tack stores and catalogs. Mesh fly sheets and leg guards, for example, can protect much of your horse's body from biting flies.

Spot-ons, Roll-ons, and Sprays

When the bugs really become bothersome, your last resorts are topical fly repellants. Most of the commercially marketed sprays, roll-ons, and spot-ons contain relatively safe, effective pyrethroids. A few insecticide-free "natural" products have a lower risk of developing resistance in insects, but they also tend to be shorter-acting and slightly less effective. Feed-through fly-control products (which you add to your horse's daily feed) contain an insecticide that kills house- and stable-fly larvae in the manure of treated horses. Like other insecticides, however, these are most effective when all of the horses on the property are on the same treatment program.

Whether the fly-control products you use are advertised as "natural" or not, always follow the directions on the label very carefully and watch for side effects, such as irritated skin and rashes. Use insecticides as judiciously as possible to reduce resistance—and keep them away from sensitive areas, such as the eyes and ears.

A fly spray misted onto your horse's body can protect him for a limited time and is relatively safe and effective. Use roll-on bug protection on his sensitive face.

Be sure to keep fly bonnets and masks as clean as possible—so they don't attract bugs themselves. When you finish your ride or bring your horse in from the pasture, dunk his bonnet or mask in water and hang it out to dry. Also periodically wash it with soapy water and rinse it well.

Chapter 20

On the Road

Today's horse world is full of equine commuters
and globetrotters journeying to shows, races,
clinics, and so on by road, rail, air, and sea.
Transporting, or "shipping," your horse from
place to place adds a certain degree of stress
to his life—particularly on longer trips. By
taking precautions and planning your trip
carefully, you can minimize your horse's risk of
travel-related accidents or illness. This chapter
will explain the basic things you need to know.

Selecting a Safe Truck and Trailer

If you plan to do the shipping yourself, acquire a safe "rig": a horse trailer and tow vehicle, or a self-powered horse van (a bread-truck-sized vehicle designed especially for horses). Just like any other automobile, your vehicles should be road-worthy, mechanically sound, and well-maintained.

Your tow vehicle should be powerful, heavy-duty, and reliable. Be sure that its towing capacity (the amount of weight the manufacturer says it can haul safely) exceeds the maximum gross vehicle weight (GVW) of your trailer when fully loaded (including horses, tack, hay, etc.) by about 1,000 pounds. Many good tow vehicles are equipped with "tow packages," which include heavy-duty suspension components, bigger or additional cooling systems, specialized electrical and brake systems, etc. Consult a reputable horse-trailer dealer about the ideal rig match.

Whatever vehicle you purchase, add extended side-view mirrors to both sides. These will reduce blind spots in traffic and help you in tricky backing situations. You'll also need good "chock blocks"—either home-made or bought from a recreational-vehicle store or horse-supply catalog—to keep your trailer tires and tongue jack from rolling or sinking into soft ground.

Hitch Up . . . Without a Hitch

Not all hitch set-ups are the same, so learn the hitching-up procedure for your particular equipment from the dealer who sold it to you. Write the steps down on paper, taking careful note of any special safety precautions. Double-check this list every time you hitch up your trailer to be sure you haven't missed any crucial steps. Always allow yourself plenty of time to hitch up—and try to plan to do it during daylight hours. Many accidents result from rigs being hastily—and improperly—hitched up.

As an added security measure, equip your rig with a "breakaway cable"—a wire connecting the tow vehicle to a battery-powered emergency-brake system in the trailer.

Traveling Clothes

Horses are usually safest and healthiest "traveling light." Trailers and vans warm up quickly when they're occupied by one or more animals. In general, it's healthier for horses to be too cold than too warm. So, even in chilly weather, you rarely need to blanket your horse on the road. (If he's been body clipped, outfit him with the minimal clothing necessary to keep him comfortable.)

Particularly for long hauls, a soft, lightweight halter with sheepskin wrapped around the noseband, cheekpieces, and crownpiece, can minimize rubs and irritation around your horse's head. Fit the halter more loosely than normal so he has plenty of room to open and close his jaw. You should be able to fit three to four fingers under the noseband and two to three fingers under the throatlatch. If you're using sheepskin pieces, adjust the halter fit after attaching them to the halter.

The most common shipping injuries result from horses stepping on themselves. To protect your horse's legs, apply thickly padded "quickie" shipping boots—which cover the horse's legs from his coronary bands to his knees or hocks—to all four legs. Overreach, or "bell," boots are also good protection for the coronary bands and heels.

Another useful piece of protection is a head bumper: a thickly padded piece of leather that fits over your horse's ears and attaches to his halter's crownpiece. This can protect him from injury if he suddenly throws his head and hits the trailer ceiling (a not-uncommon occurrence during loading and unloading).

Loading, Unloading, and Tying

There are two kinds of entrances to trailers: ramps and step-ups. Horses can learn to go up and down either one

Types of Trailers

Trailers come in two varieties: "gooseneck" and "tagalong." Gooseneck trailers extend over the rear end of the pickup truck and connect to a hitch in the middle of the truck bed. Tagalong trailers have triangular "tongues," extending in front of them at about wheel height, that connect to a hitch at the back of the tow vehicle's frame. Although goosenecks are more expensive, they're generally safer, more stable, and more maneuverable than tagalong trailers of the same size.

To be safe, always block your trailer tires with chocks before unhitching, even if the trailer is parked on the level. Never load a horse into or tie a horse to an unhitched tagalong trailer.

Before taking your horse anywhere, be sure you have a copy of his negative Coggins test. If you plan to cross state lines, he'll also need a current health certificate and, depending on the states you enter, a brand inspection and/ or proof of vaccinations. Ask your veterinarian or call the Department of Agriculture or Livestock Board in the states you'll be entering to see what paperwork you'll need on hand.

Safety is a primary concern when loading horses onto a trailer. Watch someone with plenty of experience do it before trying it yourself.

confidently. Safe, effective trailer loading and unloading requires a certain amount of skill, particularly with horses who are reticent to enter these claustrophobic-looking spaces. Ask an experienced horse person to show you how to do it properly before trying it on your own.

Once your horse is in the trailer, always close the "butt bar" (or, in the case of a slant trailer, the partition) behind him before tying him up. Snap his lead rope to the upper side ring on his halter closest to the tie ring, rather than to the ring on his chin. This will give him more head freedom and will reduce the chances of the halter shifting. Rather than tying the lead rope directly to a ring in the trailer, connect the two with a plastic cable tie or piece of baling twine that will break under pressure. Tie the rope loosely enough so that he can still lower his head to about chest-height, but not so loosely that he can reach a hoof over it.

When unloading your horse, always untie him first before removing the butt bar or partition.

Tips From the Back-Stall Driver

While you're driving, remember that your horse has to work constantly to stay on his feet in the trailer, so try not to do anything that might throw him off balance. Here are a few driving tips:

★ Accelerate and brake gradually, and take all turns slowly.

★ Don't change lanes abruptly. Remember that your rig is much longer than a normal car, so look for a big gap in traffic before switching lanes.

★ Merge into traffic slowly. Again, look for large gaps in traffic so other drivers don't have to slow down as you gradually accelerate.

★ Slow down when traveling up and down hills, particularly ones that are combined with curves in the road.

★ Steer clear of stop-and-go traffic. Plan your trips to avoid major city roads during rush hour.

★ Detour around rough, bumpy roads.

For the Long Haul

On trips longer than about six hours, plan to take 20- to 30-minute pit stops every four to six hours. Park somewhere quiet and open all of the windows completely. Ventilation in a trailer declines drastically when it's no longer in motion. Try to park in a breezy, shady spot. Untie your horse and offer him water. (Some horses don't like to drink water from unfamiliar sources, so bring along large containers of water from home.) If you can do it safely, remove soiled bedding from the trailer floor.

Travel Emergency Kit

Pack these items in your truck or trailer:

★ Extra halter and lead shank for each horse

★ Human and equine first-aid kits

★ Flashlight with fresh or rechargeable batteries

★ Jumper cables and spare fuses

★ Emergency flares

★ Jack and other tire-changing tools

★ Chock blocks (for blocking the trailer tires to prevent it from rolling)

★ Fire extinguisher

★ Tool kit

★ Cell phone and emergency phone numbers (vet, friends with trailers or local commercial shipper, tow company, etc.)

Horses who travel long distances benefit from having sheepskin-lined halters to protect against chafing and irritation.

For trips longer than 12 hours, schedule overnight stops where you can unload your horse and allow him to rest in a stall or paddock.

When you arrive at your destination, unload your horse and take him to a stall to urinate and drink water. Remove his shipping boots, etc. After about 15 minutes, take him out again for a long hand-walk/graze or turn him out in a paddock for a few hours. This is essential for helping him drain the bacteria and debris from his airways.

Check his temperature about an hour after arrival, then again several hours later. (To learn how to take your horse's temperature, go to Chapter 21.) An elevated temperature of about 102°F is normal after shipping; however, it should drop back to normal (99 to 100.5°F) within a few hours. Check his temperature daily and monitor his general health for the next two to three days to be sure he's not developing shipping fever.

Very long hauls may affect your horse's athletic performance. If you travel longer than six to eight hours, give him at least 24 hours to rest and recuperate before a competition or strenuous exercise. After trips lasting 12 hours or longer, give him two to three rest days.

Trailer Safety Checklist

Before you hit the road, check:

1. *The trailer hitch:* Is the ball properly attached and locked into place? Are the safety chains the correct length (ask an expert), properly crossed under the hitch, and securely connected to the truck? Is the power cable the proper length (shorter than the safety chains, but long enough to stay connected around turns) and looped over the hitch or a chain (so it doesn't drag on the ground), with the coupler securely connected?

2. *Adjust the trailer brakes:* Different rigs have different types of brake controllers that you must adjust to match the load you're pulling. Ask your truck or trailer dealer to go over this process with you very thoroughly when you purchase the rig.

3. *Lights:* With the help of a friend, check that *all* of the taillights.

4. *Tires:* Check the pressure on both the truck and trailer tires.

5. *Tow-vehicle fluid levels:* Top up your tanks before loading your horse.

6. At least once a year, give your trailer an entire overhaul (or hire a mechanic to do it).

Do not unload your horse from the trailer at highway rest stops. The loud noises and strange surroundings increase the risk of him breaking free and running out into traffic.

On long trips or if your horse is going to spend extra time in the trailer, be sure to tend to his needs for fresh air, food, water, and cleanliness.

Part 6

Keeping Your Horse Healthy

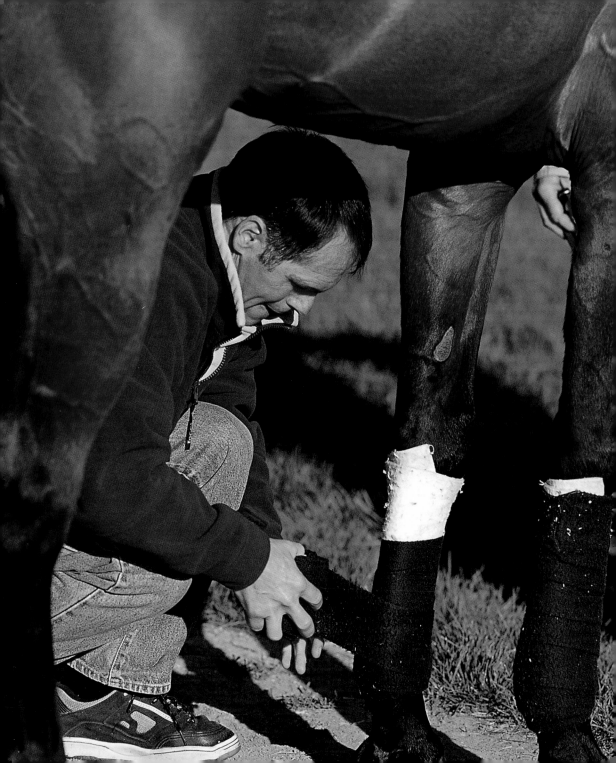

Chapter 21

Preventative Care

Keeping your horse healthy requires

a twofold approach: 1) protecting him

from serious diseases, with the help and

guidance of your veterinarian; and 2)

learning to recognize the early signs of

health problems so you can nip them

in the bud.

Vaccinations

Start by checking that your horse is up-to-date on his vaccinations. Which diseases you vaccinate against and how often you do it depends on where you live and how frequently he comes in contact with strange horses. Most vaccines must be administered initially in two to three doses spaced several weeks apart. After that, depending on the duration of the vaccine, your horse's immunity levels can be maintained with regular "boosters" given one or more times per year. Discuss vaccinating your horse against the following diseases with your veterinarian:

Eastern, Western, and Venezuelan Encephalitis, West Nile Virus

These mosquito-borne diseases all affect the nervous system and are highly fatal in unvaccinated horses. In hot, buggy climates, two to three boosters may be recommended per year. In other regions, annual boosters are best given in the spring, several weeks before mosquito season.

Equine Influenza (Flu)

As in humans, the flu is one of the most common contagious equine respiratory diseases. The average pleasure horse may only need one to two boosters per year. However, because the vaccine is relatively short-lived, frequent competitors or horses living in high-traffic barns should be vaccinated every two to four months.

Equine Herpesvirus (EHV, Rhinopneumonitis, or "rhino")

The two most serious strains of this disease, equine herpesvirus type 1 (EHV-1) and equine herpesvirus type 4 (EHV-4), cause respiratory-tract infections, abortion, neurological disorders, neonatal foal death, and ocular (eye) disease. Outbreaks are most common in young horses, particularly in busy show and race barns.

Although the respiratory form of the disease is rarely fatal, the risk for fatalities from the neurological disease is significant. Vaccination may not be necessary in mature horses who are never exposed to new horses, but annual boosters (or boosters given as frequently as every three to four months) are highly recommended in competition horses and those in heavily trafficked barns.

Tetanus

More than 80 percent of horses affected by tetanus, or "lockjaw," die. Tetanus is caused by bacterial spores entering the body through wounds (particularly puncture wounds) and lacerations. Annual boosters are recommended in all horses.

Strangles (Strep)

A highly contagious disease caused by the bacterium *Streptococcus equi*, strangles is most commonly associated with painful swelling of the lymph nodes between the jawbones, which can develop into abscesses. Although most horses recover from the disease without serious complications, some cases can be fatal. Both of the preventative vaccines available, an intramuscular injection and an intranasal vaccine, can have side effects (pain and swelling at the injection site and strangles-like symptoms, respectively). Administering them to isolated animals may be optional. However, annual vaccination is recommended for most horses.

Rabies

Rabies isn't common in all regions of the country; however, because death is inevitable in all affected horses and the disease can be transmitted from horses to humans, annual boosters are recommended.

Potomac Horse Fever

Highly fatal Potomac Horse Fever outbreaks are usually only seen in the proximity of large rivers such as the Potomac in Maryland, the Susquehanna in Pennsylvania, and the Snake River in Idaho and Wyoming. Ask your veterinarian if vaccination is advisable in your region.

Parasite Prevention

Because intestinal parasites (worms) live in the manure and dirt of virtually every pasture and paddock, all horses harbor a certain worm population in their bodies. Heavy worm infestations can cause gastrointestinal problems, weight loss, malnutrition, organ damage, and colic. A catchall term

Keeping your horse well hydrated is one of the simplest ways to promote good health.

for abdominal pain in horses, colic can result in such severe intestinal distress that it can become life-threatening. (More on this deadly disease in Chapter 22.)

Stable Management

★ Remove manure from small paddocks at least twice weekly. If possible, compost it before spreading it on larger pastures. Parasite eggs and larvae are killed by high composting temperatures. Do not harrow pastures. (Contrary to popular belief, harrowing pastures to break up manure piles and expose parasite eggs to the elements does not kill the parasites. On the other hand, allowing horses to "landscape" pastures with their natural grazing method—avoiding the grass growing out of old feces, thus creating tufts of tall grass, called "roughs," surrounded by chewed-down "lawns"—is the most effective way to minimize worm ingestion.)

★ Avoid overgrazing. Rotate and rest pastures frequently (if possible, allow other livestock, such as sheep and cattle, to graze the same pasture).

- ⋆ Remove bot eggs (tiny yellow eggs that the bot fly lays on horses' coats, usually on the lower legs).
- ⋆ Submit fecal samples to your veterinarian to analyze for parasite content. This will help you evaluate the effectiveness of your parasite-control program and determine how it needs to be adjusted, for example, to target a particular parasite species.

De-Worming Program

The two most commonly recommended equine parasite prevention programs are: 1) feeding a daily de-wormer product or 2) rotating among "families" of paste de-wormer drugs.

Because of growing concerns about worms developing resistance to the drugs we use against them, experts advise working closely with your veterinarian to determine what drugs to use and how frequently to use them in your horse's specific program. Use fecal egg counts (submitting manure samples to your veterinarian about two to three weeks after each drug administration) to determine how infested your horse is with parasites and to find out how effectively the drugs are working. To help minimize drug resistance, give all of the horses on your property the same drug at the same time. If you feed a daily de-wormer, supplement biannually with a paste macrocyclic lactone product. To insure tapeworm removal in either program, include a praziquantel dose once yearly.

Down the Hatch!

As a horse owner, you'll have to get a lot of different messy medications down your horse's throat. The goal is always to get more in his mouth than on your clothes.

Signs of parasite infestation may include a dull, rough coat, tail rubbing, depression, loss of appetite, and diarrhea. Fortunately, good stable management and a regular de-worming program with effective anthelmintics (drugs that kill worms) can minimize these effects.

One way to control parasites is by periodically administering de-wormer medications via an oral paste syringe.

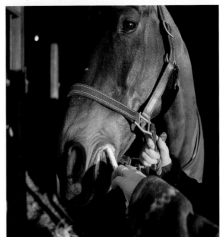

Which Worms?

The intestinal parasites that plague horses include:
* large strongyles
* small strongyles (bloodworms)
* ascarids (roundworms)
* pinworms
* bots
* tapeworms
* threadworms
* lungworms

Of these, the most dangerous are small strongyles and tapeworms.

Unlike us, horses can only breathe through their noses. This means that they can't choke on food that "goes down the wrong tube" the way we can. Horses also can't vomit. So, if your horse is feeling sick to his tummy, you'll have to look for signs other than "tossed cookies." Toxic plants and substances are doubly dangerous for horses because we can't induce them to vomit back up things they ingest.

The following tips should make it easier and more successful for you to do this.

Paste de-wormers: To determine the correct dose for your horse, purchase a weight-measuring tape from your local feed store. Wrap this around your horse's belly, about where the girth goes, to estimate his weight. Then, set the adjusting ring on the de-wormer syringe to the appropriate dosage and remove the cap. Try to administer the de-wormer when your horse doesn't have any hay, grass, or grain in his mouth—which makes it easier for him to lump the medication with the food and spit it out.

Standing on your horse's left side, reach your right hand under his jaw and over the bridge of his nose to hold his head in place. With your left hand, place the tip of the syringe into the corner of his mouth and, as he opens his mouth, push it toward the back of his tongue. Depress the plunger with your thumb.

As you remove it, try to cup one hand under your horse's chin and elevate his head for a moment. This may help to make him swallow—rather than spit out—the medication. If he does spit it out (and every horse does at one time or another), it's good to have a spare syringe on hand to repeat the dose. With de-wormers, it's always better to slightly overdose than to underdose.

Some pill medications can be administered in a similar way with a large plastic syringe (ask your veterinarian for one). Cut the plastic tip off the end of the syringe so the medication can be squeezed out more easily. Crush the pills with a mortar and pestle or—if the pills will dissolve—dissolve them in a small amount of warm water. Then, mix them with applesauce and/or molasses. Pour this mixture into the top of the syringe and administer it just as you would a de-wormer.

More palatable medications can sometimes be added to a horse's grain meal. Mix the medication into the grain thoroughly—smart horses can sniff out the medication and carefully eat around it. To make the mixture even tastier, consider adding molasses, carrots, and/or apples. Always check afterward to see if your horse finished his meal, and thus received the full recommended dose.

Tend to the Teeth

Every horse should have regular annual dental care. Because of the way their teeth wear from chewing, all horses develop sharp edges on their teeth that need to be "floated" (smoothed away). Schedule annual visits with a qualified veterinarian or certified equine dental technician.

If your horse shows signs of dental distress—dropping grain out of his mouth; excessive salivation and/or tilting the head while eating; "quidding" (dropping chewed-up clumps of hay or grass out of his mouth); a foul smell in his mouth; or bitting problems, such as resistance to the bridle and head-tossing—schedule more frequent dental care.

Monitor Your Horse for Good Health

Develop a habit of monitoring your horse's health from day to day, so you'll know immediately when problems begin to arise:

Signs of Good Health

⋆ Bright and shiny coat

⋆ "Bright" eye and good general attitude and expression

⋆ Good hydration. To test this, gently pinch a fold of

De-Worming Drug Families

Many anthelmintic (de-worming) drugs are distributed under different brand names, so if you use a rotating program, be sure to rotate the specific drugs, rather than just the brands.

⋆ Benzimidazoles: fenbendazole, oxibendazole, and oxfendazole
⋆ Macrocyclic lactones: ivermectin and moxidectin
⋆ Piperazine
⋆ Pyrantel pamoate
⋆ Pyrantel tartrate (daily)
⋆ Praziquantel (the only anthelmintic currently approved for use against tapeworms)

Although most of these drugs are safe to use on any horse, moxidectin is extremely potent and should only be used on horses already in a routine de-worming program. Using it on a horse with a heavy parasite infestation can cause severe gastrointestinal distress. If you don't know a horse's de-worming history, use other drugs for several rotations before treating him with moxidectin.

Horses need regular dental care by a qualified veterinarian or equine dental technician to protect against any problems of the teeth or mouth.

your horse's skin on his neck between your thumb and fingers. Pull the skin about an inch from his body and then release it. In a well-hydrated horse, the skin should sink quickly back into place. If your horse is dehydrated, the fold of skin may take several seconds to disappear.

⋆ Good mucus-membrane color. Gently grasp your horse's upper lip and lift it up until you can see his gums. They should be a nice pink color (not pale, whitish, dark red, or bluish) and moist to the touch. Press a finger firmly on the gum line, and then remove it quickly. The spot should look almost white at first, but should return to its normal pink color within about two seconds. This is called capillary refill time. Anything longer than about two seconds may be a sign of trouble. (Don't try this with a horse you don't know or one with a reputation for biting.)

⋆ Good gut sounds. Healthy horses produce a lot of rumbling, gurgling, and tinkling noises in their intestines. You can often hear them simply by resting an ear against your horse's flank, in front of and below the point of the hip (only do this with a tolerant horse who you trust not to kick you), but a stethoscope makes it even easier. Hold it against both sides of the flank and underneath his chest, about where the girth goes. Count the sounds as you watch the seconds on your watch. You should hear at least two gurgles or rumbles in the space of about a minute.

⋆ Normal potty patterns. Your horse's manure may vary somewhat with changes in his diet. However, it should generally form soft, round balls ("road apples"). Unlike with humans, you can't judge a horse's bladder health by the color of his urine. (The high calcium content in a horse's diet can make his normal urine very thick and dark—sometimes almost brown). Instead, try to monitor how frequently he urinates and how much urine he normally produces.

> Don't be surprised if your veterinarian or dentist recommends mildly sedating or tranquilizing your horse for his dental treatment. This is the best way to get him to stand still and say "Ahhh" for the length of time it takes to float his big mouthful of teeth properly.

Signs of Poor Health

⋆ Dull, rough coat

⋆ Sweating (not caused by exercise or extreme heat)

⋆ Shaking/trembling

⋆ Loss of appetite

⋆ Uncharacteristic behavior: depression, lethargy, irritability, pacing, restlessness, etc.

⋆ Thick, discolored nasal discharge

⋆ Runny, gooey eyes

⋆ Chronic coughing

⋆ Dehydration (see hydration test above)

⋆ Poor mucus membrane color (see above)

⋆ No gut signs or an excessive amount of sounds

⋆ Abnormal potty patterns. Signs of bladder and/or kidney disease include squatting to urinate during exercise, acting generally uncomfortable, exhibiting pain during exercise, showing discomfort in the hind end, urinating more frequently than normal, but in smaller amounts, standing in a urinating position without urinating,

drinking noticeably more water, and producing either much larger or smaller amounts of urine than usual. Extremely hard, dry manure can be a sign of dehydration or colic. Long periods of time between bowel movements, very loose bowel movements, and diarrhea can also be signs of illness.

★ Coordination problems (excessive stumbling, hind-end weakness, etc.)

★ Changes in daily routine. Get to know your horse's habits. When does he normally lie down to sleep? During what times of day is he most and least active? Does he eat his meals with gusto or just pick at them? How does he behave when you turn him out to pasture? Obvious, unexplainable changes in these "norms" can indicate the onset of a health problem.

Consult your veterinarian immediately if you notice any serious signs of poor health or if mild signs persist longer than 24 hours or worsen.

Vital Signs

One of the best ways to evaluate your horse's health—and to monitor his fitness level during a conditioning program—is to check his TPR (temperature, pulse, and respiration). To establish baseline numbers to which you can refer later, practice "taking his vitals" when he's at rest and healthy. (Always put a halter or bridle on your horse to control him while you're taking his vitals.)

Hot, Cold, or Just Right?

To take your horse's temperature, you'll need a thermometer, preferably the soft, plastic, digital kind (available at drug stores and through horse-supply catalogs) with a small hole on the end to which you can attach a

It's important for others in your barn to know what's going on with your horse, too. Keeping a chart outside your horse's stall can be extremely helpful.

Left: Paying close attention to your horse's daily routine, including how he behaves outside and inside, what he likes to do, how much he eats and drinks, etc., will help you monitor his overall health.

long piece of yarn or thread. Knot a clothespin or small clamp to the end of the yarn so you can attach the thermometer to the tail while it's in use (so it won't get lost in bedding or manure if it falls out).

If you're using a glass thermometer, shake it until it reads below 95°F. Then cover the business end with Vaseline or KY Jelly. Standing to the side of your horse, lift his tail with one hand and gently insert the thermometer into his anus. Clamp the string to his tail and wait three to five minutes (for a glass thermometer) or a minute or so (for a digital thermometer). Then remove the thermometer, wipe it clean with a cloth and read the temperature.

A normal rectal temperature should be between 98 and 101.5°F. Slightly elevated temperatures on warm days or immediately after exercise or trailering are normal. At rest, a temperature above 101°F can indicate an infection, severe dehydration, or toxic condition within the body. A temperature below 98°F may indicate shock. In either case, consult your veterinarian immediately.

Every Breath He Takes

To measure your horse's respiratory rate, stand by his side and watch his flanks expand and contract. If you're having trouble seeing the movement in his flanks, hold one hand in front of his nostrils and try to feel the air against your skin as he exhales. Meanwhile, hold a watch that displays seconds. Count the number of breaths he takes in 15 seconds, then multiply that by four to determine his breaths per minute.

A normal respiratory rate at rest should be 12 to 24 breaths per minute. More rapid, shallow breathing may be a sign of pain, fever, or other illness—and reason to call the vet.

Rate His Heart

To measure your horse's heart rate, or pulse, you can try to feel it in the artery that crosses the bottom of his jawbone. Doing this well takes practice, however, so you may be better off buying an inexpensive stethoscope (from a drug store or horse-supply catalog). Press the head of the stethoscope on the left side of your horse's chest, just behind his elbow (about where the girth goes). Each "lub-dub" you hear is one heartbeat. Using your watch again, count the number of beats you hear in 15 seconds. Multiply this by four to get his resting pulse.

A normal horse has a resting pulse, or heart rate, of 30 to 40 beats per minute. A rate from 40 to 60 in a horse who hasn't just exercised can indicate pain—and anything above 60 may indicate dehydration or shock. Call the veterinarian immediately!

Keep Records

Keep a daily journal for your horse. Record his general attitude, feed and hay ration, turn-out and exercise details. If you have the time, take his vital signs (at least his temperature) daily, so you'll notice any change immediately. Note environmental and weather changes, too. You might not see a connection between them and a change in your horse's health until looking back at your record book later. But these notes may prove invaluable for predicting and preventing future problems.

Paying attention to and noting anything unusual about your horse from day to day is one of the best ways to stay on top of his overall health.

Chapter 22

Common Equine Ailments

Compared to us, horses are relatively

healthy creatures. Your horse may go years

without showing signs of a cold, tummy

ache, or other "bug." However, in addition

to the diseases described in the last

chapter, there are several equine-specific

ailments, ranging from mildly threatening

to potentially fatal, that you and your

veterinarian need to watch out for.

Colic – The #1 Killer

Even if you haven't spent much time around horse people, you'll sense a sudden chill in the air around them if someone mentions the word "colic." A broad term for abdominal pain, this frightening condition can occur in horses of any age, sex, or breed, and can progress rapidly from mild discomfort to severe pain. There are three basic kinds of colic:

1. An "impaction" happens when food builds up in one part of the intestine, causing partial or complete blockage. If the blockage isn't dislodged promptly, it can cause severe pain and serious damage.

2. "Gas colic" results from excess gas in the intestines (due to sudden dietary change or prolonged periods between meals), which can cause mild to severe discomfort.

3. The most fatal form of colic, "twisted gut" occurs when the intestine twists back on itself, cutting off the blood flow to the intestinal tissue. (Contrary to popular belief, twists are usually caused by too much gas accumulation in the large colon, not by horses rolling.) Twists rarely correct themselves, so they usually need to be surgically corrected. Only about half of horses with completely twisted colons survive surgery.

Surgery for severe cases involves opening the horse's abdomen, readjusting the intestines, and sometimes cutting out damaged tissue before sewing the remaining sections back in place. Of the horses who make it to the operating table, 75 to 80 percent survive the procedure. Not only is this experience traumatic and emotionally draining for a horse owner, it can also be financially devastating. From the first vet call to the final surgery aftercare visit, bills for one colic episode can add up to several thousand dollars. (A good equine insurance policy may cover much of the cost of colic surgery. See Chapter 14.)

Signs of Possible Colic:

* Loss of appetite
* Unusually long periods of time between bowel movements

* Turning head to look at or nip the sides
* Pawing at the ground
* Repeatedly getting up and down
* Excessive rolling
* "Parking" the body—standing with the front legs stretched out in front and the hind legs stretched out behind
* Pained, uncomfortable expression (distant or worried look in the eyes, ears flopped to sides or backward, tension around mouth)
* Nose curled up in the Flehmen response (see Chapter 2)
* Signs of more severe pain: thrashing around the stall, kicking at sides, rolling violently, and breaking into a sweat

If you suspect that your horse may be colicking, check his vital signs and listen for gut sounds (review Chapter 21). Examine his surroundings: Does the stall bedding look more disorderly than normal? Is there grain leftover from his last meal? Are there less manure piles than usual? Is your horse lying down at an uncharacteristic time of day? If he is, make some noise to get him back on his feet, then leave him alone in his stall for 10 to 15 minutes. When you return, if he's behaving normally, he's probably okay. If he's lying down again, there may be a problem.

Ask your veterinarian if he or she prefers that you walk your horse while you wait for his or her arrival. Some veterinarians recommend allowing a colicky horse to rest quietly in his stall, unless he's rolling so violently that he risks hurting himself. Others encourage some walking, but not for longer than about 90 minutes, which can exhaust his strength.

Take Action Now!

Although no horse is 100 percent safe from colic, the

> **Be Alert for Early Signs of Colic**
>
> The earlier you catch a mild colic, the better chance you have of preventing it from turning it into something serious. Rather than waiting hours to see if your horse's condition improves, if you notice anything significantly out of the ordinary, consult your veterinarian. He or she would rather spend a few minutes on an unnecessary call or visit than be contacted too late to save a horse in distress.

way you feed and care for your horse can greatly reduce his chances of getting it. Dehydration, high-starch diets, lack of exercise/turn-out, intestinal parasites (even in foals), and large, infrequent meals are all common causes of colic. Stress, changes in environment, and climate changes can also contribute to colic.

Sand Colic

In desert and coastal areas (Florida, the Carolinas, California, etc.) and other regions with particularly sandy soil, excessive sand ingestion can cause build-up in the intestines that leads to colic. The victim usually eats sand unintentionally, either when it's mixed in with his food or when he's rooting for stray bits of grass or hay. The best preventive measures to take are:

★ Feeding hay in a trough-like feeder or on a large rubber mat on the ground

★ Dividing and rotating pastures so they're not overgrazed

★ Feeding free-choice (a constant supply of) hay or dividing it into three to four meals per day

★ Increasing your horse's daily hay portion to at least 2.5 percent of his body weight (For example, feeding a 1,000-pound horse 25 pounds of hay per day.) This will not only keep your horse too busy to root through the sandy ground, but the natural fiber will also help to remove much of the sand in his gut.

Ulcers

Studies show that 60 percent of show horses and 90 percent of racehorses suffer from gastric (stomach) ulcers. Many performance problems once blamed on behavioral

Is He Pooping Sand?

To find out if your horse is ingesting too much sand, ask your veterinarian to perform a fecal sedimentation test. If the test shows that his manure contains a significant amount of sand, he or she may recommend adding psyllium, a laxative substance derived from plants, to his diet.

Left: Your veterinarian may suggest you walk your horse while you're waiting for him or her to arrive. Taking a friend along may keep both of you calmer.

257

issues, sore backs, and other hard-to-diagnose causes are now believed to be linked to ulcer discomfort.

Like colic, ulcers can be significantly minimized with good horse management. The primary causes are long periods between meals (horses constantly produce acid in their stomachs so, without food to digest, the acid begins to eat away at the stomach lining), unrelenting training and competition schedules, and stressful lifestyles. Review the feeding recommendations in Chapter 18 and take the following precautions.

Vary your horse's training schedule. Rather than drilling him day after day with high-intensity workouts, alternate them with easier, low-intensity sessions.

Try to lower his stress levels at competitions. Whenever possible, return him to his stall and leave him alone to rest and relax.

If your veterinarian diagnoses ulcers, he or she will probably recommend putting your horse on a course of omeprazole (the only drug currently known to treat ulcers effectively). As the condition improves, you may want to keep him on a maintenance dose of the drug or use it periodically at high-stress times (before competitions, etc.)

Hard training schedules, long periods between meals, and other stresses can contribute to ulcers in horses.

Equine Protozoal Myeloencephalitis (EPM)

The opossum is the primary carrier of the *Sarcocystis neurona* organism that causes this progressively debilitating neurological disease. Infected horses show a variety of symptoms ranging from unusual lameness and breathing trouble to difficulty walking, standing, or swallowing, and seizures. Consult your veterinarian immediately if you notice any of these signs.

Respiratory Problems

Chapter 21 described some of the common respiratory problems against which you can vaccinate your horse. Flu, rhino, and strangles can all cause runny nose, fever, depression, and loss of appetite. Immediate, proper care may stop these problems from developing into more serious infections. Always consult your veterinarian when you first notice symptoms.

Whereas most temporary respiratory diseases occur in horses two years of age or younger, mature horses are more vulnerable to chronic breathing problems. Allergies, for instance, can contribute to sinus problems and airway irritation that cause runny nose, cough, and general discomfort.

The most common chronic respiratory disease in adult horses is Recurrent Airway Obstruction (RAO), or "heaves." Similar to asthma in humans, heaves is characterized by periodic breathing difficulty caused by inflammation and constriction of the lower airways. Other signs include cough, nasal discharge, flared nostrils, exercise intolerance (reluctance to perform at higher intensity levels or for longer duration) and, in severe cases, weight loss.

Roaring Like a Lion

Different horses make different types of blowing sounds in their noses and throats as they exercise, particularly while galloping fast. The worst sounds you'll hear come from "roarers," horses suffering from some form of airway interference. Their very loud, distinctive sound comes from either a vocal cord collapsing into the airway, displacement of the soft palate, or epiglottis entrapment (the soft palate and epiglottis are two structures located in the back of the throat). Although mild cases of these conditions often cause no problem or pain in low-level performance and pleasure horses, severe cases can be performance-limiting.

Over time, the continually labored breathing results in a "heave line": a defined ridge of overdeveloped muscle along the horse's ribcage, angling back and up toward his flanks.

Handling Heaves

Heaves is most commonly seen in stabled horses who are exposed to irritating airborne particles—primarily mold—from hay and bedding. Full-time outdoor living on good pasture (rather than hay) is usually the best treatment. If that's not feasible, try to turn your horse out as much as possible. Meanwhile, try to reduce all sources of airborne particles by:

* Throwing out moldy hay and bedding
* Soaking hay with water before feeding
* Cleaning stalls more frequently and using less dusty, more absorbent bedding
* Improving ventilation in the barn (opening windows, etc.)
* Sprinkling water on dusty arenas
* Vacuuming or sweeping the barn aisle, rather than using an electric blower

Skin Problems

Regular grooming, a good de-worming program, swift treatment of wounds, and careful inspection of your horse's coat can prevent or catch most skin problems in the early stages before they become serious. Here are some of the most common ones:

Rain Rot, or Rain Scald

In hot, humid climates, excessive dampness in a horse's coat encourages the growth of bacteria on his skin. Dry, crusty scabs often form on the horse's back. They're not usually itchy or painful and can often be gently curried or shampooed away. More severe cases, however, can lead to infection. Contact your veterinarian if the condition doesn't resolve within two weeks.

Scratches ("Dew Poisoning," Grease Heel, or Cracked Heel)

Moisture is the main culprit in this common, often chronic skin problem that develops in usually one or both hind legs. Standing in a wet pasture or unsanitary paddocks causes a chain reaction of skin softening, mite invasion, staph infection and, eventually, fungal infection. As the condition progresses, crusty, scabby bumps appear in the area between the fetlocks (ankles) and heels. When the bumps break open, they can cause pain, bleeding, and even lameness. The skin in the region can become inflamed and irritated. In the absence of treatment, severe infection and lameness can result. Effective treatment involves:

★ Clipping the hair in the region.

★ Gently washing the affected area with an antibacterial solution.

★ Applying a combination of anti-fungal, anti-bacterial, anti-inflammatory, and anti-parasitic topical medications. (Ask your veterinarian for his or her favorite mixture.)

★ Changing your horse's environment: Get him out of the wet! Bed his stall with at least two feet of dry, absorbent bedding (avoid using straw, which can be abrasive on the tender skin and often has a very high fungal content), and turn him out when the pasture isn't muddy or heavy with dew.

Photosensitization

Often mistaken for scratches, this condition results when the horse's body deposits certain substances in his diet (rich alfalfa or clover) in the skin where they react with sunlight, causing a burn. A patch of scabby crud results in the area. Unlike scratches, photosensitization only occurs on white legs. Removing alfalfa and clover from your horse's diet and applying sunblock to his legs can help. However, more severe cases may require medication provided by your veterinarian.

Sunburn

Yes, horses can get sunburn, too—especially light-skinned horses or horses with pink noses and face markings. Intense sun exposure can cause red, irritated skin, which can then blister and peel. If you know your horse may be prone to sunburn, keep him inside during the sunniest hours of the day, put on a white fly mask and fly sheet, or apply regular human sunblock to his most vulnerable areas before he goes out.

While horses do best with plenty of pasture time, giving it to them also increases their exposure to the harmful effects of the sun as well as parasites.

Ticks, Lice, Mange, and Pinworms

All of these parasites can cause itching, discomfort, and hair loss. A common sign of infestation is a horse backing up against walls and fences to rub his tail—or leaning against or putting his nose through fence rails to rub his mane. Look carefully through the mane and tail for ticks and wash both with disinfectant soap. Reevaluate his de-worming program to be sure he's being adequately protected against pinworms. If the problem persists or worsens, consult your veterinarian about the possibility of and treatment for lice or mange (mite) infestation.

Ringworm

This condition is actually caused by a fungus, not a worm. It spreads from horse to horse, producing round, itchy skin lesions that eventually form blisters that break and leave scabs. If your veterinarian diagnoses this highly contagious disease, disinfect all of your horse's brushes and saddle pads and keep them separate from other horses until the condition resolves.

Tumors

Skin tumors are one of the most common equine cancers. Malignant (cancerous) tumors, called squamous cell carcinomas, often occur around the eyes or sheath of light-skinned horses. Growths called melanomas, most commonly seen under the tails of gray horses, can also be fatal. Benign sarcoids can occur around the eyes, muzzle, belly, and under the tailhead. Gray horses are more prone to sarcoids than dark-colored horses. Unlike in humans, though, sarcoids are rarely fatal.

Proud Flesh

Sometimes, rather than healing normally, excessive granular (scar) tissue in a wound grows above the normal skin surface, inhibiting the wound edges from closing. This can delay healing significantly. Proud flesh is more common in the lower legs, where blood flow is limited. If your horse develops it on a wound, your veterinarian may need to debride (scrape away) the extra granular tissue to get the healing back on the right track.

Hives

Just like humans, horses can develop skin rashes and hives from contact or exposure to allergens, irritants, and chemicals. Overuse of fly sprays and other horse-care products can aggravate the problem. Some allergic conditions, left untreated, can lead to hair loss, secondary infections, and thickened, wrinkled skin. If you notice large, flat, circular swellings (wheals), redness, and/or significant itching, consult your veterinarian.

Eye Problems

Excessive tearing, swelling, redness, pain, and sensitivity (closing the eye frequently or avoiding being touched in the area) in the eyes can indicate a corneal scratch or deeper cut, a foreign body stuck in the eye, or infection.

If symptoms occur in both eyes, it's more likely conjunctivitis (inflammation of the mucous membrane around the eye caused by dust, flies, fly spray, and exposure to other irritants and allergens) or another type of infection, such as Equine Recurrent Uveitis (ERU or "moonblindness"). Symptoms of ERU, which may also include photophobia (squinting in moderate to bright light), can appear and disappear periodically. This chronic condition is caused by multiple factors and isn't easy to cure permanently.

Horses can also suffer from cataracts—whitish, opaque spots on the

Be alert to any abnormalities in or around your horse's eyes.

ocular lens—which can cause serious visual impairment or blindness. In many cases, however, cataracts can be surgically removed.

Many untreated minor eye problems can progress to severe infections resulting in vision impairment and even blindness. So, consult your veterinarian immediately if you notice any of the above symptoms in your horse's eyes.

Laminitis/Founder

Although this disease manifests in the hooves, causing severe pain and sometimes even structural changes, the initial trigger is often believed to result from a traumatic system overload, including a reaction to a drug, colic surgery, repeated concussion on hard surfaces, overeating grain, and hormonal imbalances, such as a pituitary-gland disorder.

The exact mechanism of the disease is still being studied, but the general belief is that systemic trauma is somehow translated to inflammation of certain sensitive structures in the feet. Since the hoof walls can't expand to accommodate this inflammation, the swelling causes tremendous pain. Horses suffering from acute laminitis, therefore, show mild to severe lameness, often rocking back on their hind legs or lying down to relieve the pressure on their front feet.

Chronic laminitis can cause permanent changes to the hoof structure and blood supply, which can make a horse lame for life. It's very important, therefore, to have any possible case of acute laminitis addressed immediately by a veterinarian.

Lyme Disease

The same disease that deer ticks transfer to humans, dogs, and other animals can occasionally strike horses as well. Caused by the bacterium *Borrelia burgdorferi*, Lyme disease is often characterized by subtle lameness in one or more legs, overall stiffness, and behavioral changes. It is more common in areas such as the northeastern and mid-Atlantic states, where a greater proportion of ticks carry the bacteria.

Only ten percent of horses infected with *Borrelia burgdorferi* show symptoms of Lyme disease. A blood test can indicate whether or not your horse has been exposed to the bacteria, but it can't determine whether or not his symptoms are indeed related to Lyme disease. If your veterinarian decides that the combination of positive test results and a clinical examination support a diagnosis of the disease, he can treat it with antibiotics and, in some cases, anti-inflammatory medication. Response to therapy is usually seen in the first two to five days. No vaccination against Lyme disease is available yet for horses.

Tying-Up

Tying-up is also referred to as azoturia, Monday morning disease, or exertional rhabdomyolysis. This condition can occur when a horse's workload suddenly increases from little or no training to intense, long-lasting work. Mild cases cause abnormal, stiff, or stilted gaits, and soreness in the hindlimbs and back. More severe cases involve extreme cramping in the back muscles and a reluctance to move. Forcing a horse to continue moving may cause serious muscle damage.

The fastest way to repair the damage already done to the muscles is to give your horse immediate rest and call your veterinarian, who will probably administer intravenous fluids to replace his fluid and electrolyte levels as soon as possible.

Causes & Care

Diet, genetics, and hormones may also play a part in this condition. Some horses (particularly high-strung, sensitive types) seem to be more prone to tying-up than others. To minimize chances of your horse tying up:

★ Stick to a realistic, fair conditioning schedule, only increasing the intensity of work when you know your horse is prepared for it.

★ Change his grain to a low-carbohydrate, high-fat ("high energy") feed and reduce grain meals by half on his days off.

★ Be sure he always has clean, fresh water available. In hot weather, consider adding electrolytes to his diet.

Chapter 23

Hoof and Leg Care

One of the most common sayings in the equine world is: "No hoof, no horse." The majority of soundness problems that interfere with performance originate in the foot. So, the more you know about caring for your horse's hooves—as well as his legs—the longer and more successful his career will be.

Healthy Hooves

A healthy hoof should have smooth, uncracked walls, a thick, concave sole, and broad, fleshy-looking heels and frog. Like your fingernails, hooves should contain enough moisture to be resistant to chipping and cracking, but not so much that they're soft and mushy.

You can do several things to promote healthy hooves:

* Pick out your horse's hooves daily, removing dirt, manure, rocks, gravel, etc.
* Keep his stall as clean, dry, and well-bedded as possible. Moist, dirty stalls are hotbeds for hoof-damaging bacteria.
* If possible, limit turn-out and exercise when conditions are extremely wet or muddy.
* Avoid frequent bathing (which can dry hooves out) or, if you must bathe, apply a hoof-moisturizing product beforehand, then dry the hooves and lower legs well with a towel afterward.

Standing in wet or muddy areas for too long can affect hoof health.

★ Schedule regular farrier (blacksmith) visits every four to six weeks. In between visits, consult him or her about any unusual changes in the hooves—cracks, bruises, loose shoes, etc.

Why Shoes?

Hooves grow from the top down, starting at the coronary band (which is similar to your fingernail cuticles). They can grow at a rate of up to three-eighths of an inch per month. In the wild, horses naturally wear down the edges of their hooves at a similar rate, so the hooves maintain a relatively constant length. Domestic horses need a little help with this, especially if they wear shoes, which prevent the hoof edges from wearing down naturally.

Without the support and protection of durable metal shoes, many horses' hooves aren't strong enough to stand up to the concussive forces and wear and tear to which we expose them. Some horses have thin, weak walls and soles, or other undesirable conformation, which makes them prone to soreness, cracking, and bruising. Shoes are a must for these horses when they're in training.

Your farrier shapes the shoe to fit your horse's foot, then attaches it by hammering nails into the insensitive outer part of the hoof. Unless he misplaces a nail, the process should be entirely painless for your horse.

Balancing Act

Part of your farrier's job is to restore the hoof angle to its natural balance. No two horses are built exactly the same, so the "ideal balance" varies from horse to horse. An improperly balanced hoof will strike the ground unevenly, loading more force on one area. Over time, this will cause

The "Weak White Foot" Myth

One of the old wives' tales passed on through generations of horse people is that white hooves are weaker than dark hooves. In fact, there is no difference in their chemical makeup or structure, other than the added pigment in the outer layer of dark hooves that gives them their color. Because the contrast is more obvious in white hooves, people tend to pay more attention to cracks and bruises in them. Dark hooves experience the same number of cracks and bruises-- they're just harder to see!

In certain sports, special shoes are necessary to provide more or less traction. For instance, in reining, a smooth shoe allows a horse to slide farther in his sliding stop. In jumping and eventing, special caulks, or "studs," provide extra grip for taking off and landing over obstacles.

If you do any kind of competitive riding with your horse, he will probably need the support and protection of shoes—and they must be put on and maintained properly.

a decrease in blood flow to that area, which will lead to more serious soundness problems.

To ensure that your horse's feet are properly balanced, your veterinarian or farrier may recommend taking x-rays. These will show whether or not the angle of the coffin bone (one of the bones inside the hoof) matches the angles of the hoof capsule and the pastern bone. A mismatch can indicate improper shoeing or a "rotated coffin bone"—a sign of serious hoof disease.

If the Shoe Fits . . . It Won't in Six Weeks

No matter how well your farrier balances your horse's hooves at shoeing time, the balance will change over time. Hooves spread as they grow, eventually expanding beyond the edges of the shoes, so the shoes no longer support the entire surface area of the hooves. Too-small shoes put pressure on the heels and quarters (sides of the foot), causing bruising, heel pain, and damage to the internal hoof structures. To avoid these

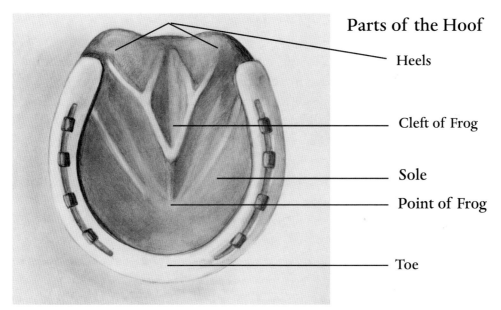

Parts of the Hoof

— Heels

— Cleft of Frog

— Sole
— Point of Frog

— Toe

problems and to minimize the destructive forces caused by imbalances, schedule regular farrier visits. (Growth rates vary. Ask your farrier the ideal interval between shoeings for your particular horse.)

Shoeing for Showing

Before starting a new show season, try to schedule to have your horse shod approximately two weeks before each show. This gives you a safety margin, in case he experiences any soreness or problems caused by a shoeing mistake. It also ensures that the hoof angles will still be in good balance and the shoes will be relatively snug. Also, ask your regular farrier to make you a spare set of shoes to take to shows. Most shows have a farrier available on the grounds to perform emergency duties, such as replacing thrown shoes. Having the right type of shoe already shaped to fit your horse's foot can save time and energy should he lose a shoe during a competition.

> **Be Farrier-Friendly**
>
> Horseshoeing is hard, physically taxing work, so be nice to your farrier! Schedule appointments well ahead of time and give him a comfortable place to work that has good natural or plenty of artificial light; level, non-slip, flooring; protection from cold wind, hot sun, and bugs; and no clutter (wheelbarrows, etc.) that the farrier or horse might bump into.

Shoeing Terms

Modern shoeing is a complicated science. To help you understand what your farrier is doing there under your horse's belly, here are some good terms to learn:

Clinches – The point of each nail exits the hoof wall about an inch or so up from the foot surface. Your farrier will pinch off the protruding nail, bend it over, and smooth it flush with the hoof wall. The resulting smoothed-off nails are called "clinches."

Clips – Half-moon shaped metal pieces extending up from the outside of the shoe to help hold it in place on the hoof. Farriers may either use a toe clip, centered in the front of the shoe, or quarter clips, placed on the sides.

Flare – Uneven growth in the hoof can result in certain areas "flaring" out more than others. Your farrier will trim away flares to return the hoof to its normal shape.

Hot shoeing – Before the invention of mass-produced pre-made shoes, farriers used hot forges to soften and shape handmade horseshoes, and then applied the shoes to the hooves hot. Now, with more than 500 styles of pre-made shoes available, farriers can choose the correct shoe for almost any situation and fit it to the horse with a relatively small amount of shaping adjustment. In the rare cases where no pre-made shoe will meet the needs of a horse, a farrier can use traditional hot shoeing to shape homemade shoes.

Because hot shoes are easier to shape, many farriers prefer to heat up pre-made shoes before applying them. However, correctly adjusted and flattened, a cold-applied shoe is just as effective as a hot-applied shoe, so there is no reason to prefer one method over the other, so long as your farrier is skilled at the method he uses.

Pricked foot, quicked foot, close nail – When a farrier hammers a nail into or very close to the sensitive structures of the hoof. This can be painful for the horse and may open the door to bacterial infection.

Underrun heels – The toes are allowed to grow exceedingly long and start to flatten out like pancakes. Looking from the side, you may see a "dish" (concave curve) in the front edge of the hoof. This unnatural balance adds stress to the tendons, ligaments, and internal structures of the foot.

Pads

Thin rubber or plastic pads attached between the hoof and shoe protect the frog and sole from sharp rocks and reduce some of the concussion of working on hard ground. However, pads can trap moisture and bacteria against the horse's foot, causing it to soften (and weaken) and making it vulnerable to infections. They also interfere with the frog's natural shock-absorbing mechanism.

Most farriers don't recommend long-term use of traditional pads. New "pour-on" pads, on the other hand, create an impermeable connection between the pad and the hoof. They're made of liquid urethane that turns into a resilient, cushion-like layer after being applied to the bottom of the hoof.

Going Barefoot

Year-round shoeing can take its toll on horses with thin or weak walls. Old nail holes can gradually contribute to cracks and chips. To give these holes time to grow out, it's often helpful to "pull" the shoes at the end of your riding or competition season and give your horse some time to wander around his pasture barefoot. The natural contact between the hoof surface and a soft, springy turf can encourage new, healthy growth that will make shoeing easier next season. In snowy climates, bare feet actually provide better traction through the winter than plain shoes. (However, if the snow frequently melts and freezes into ice, the hard footing can contribute to sore feet.)

Not all horses have strong enough hooves to go barefoot, particularly if they live and work on hard, rocky ground. Ask your farrier if a vacation from shoes would be appropriate for your particular horse. While he is barefoot, continue scheduling appointments for your farrier to even out the rough edges of his hooves and correct any imbalances.

Depending on what kind of riding you do and how strong your horses' hooves are, he may need shoes only on his front feet. Because the front feet experience more concussion than the hind feet, they usually require more support and protection. Some horses have such strong feet that they can

Glue-On Shoes!

Special acrylic "glue-on" shoes are a great way to protect a horse's hooves while giving his walls a break from the damage caused by nail holes. A farrier may recommend using glue-on shoes for several months to help a horse with thin, weak walls grow enough new, healthy foot to hold nails again. A glue-on shoe can stay on for as long as six weeks, even if the horse is working or turned out in wet, muddy conditions.

273

train and compete up to a certain level entirely barefoot. To maintain the lateral balance in your horse's legs, never shoe just one front foot or one hind foot.

Hoof Ailments
Abscess

Once a bruise or foreign object (nail, piece of wire, metal, dirt, bacteria, etc.) penetrates the tough, protective hoof capsule, it can wreak havoc in the internal structures. Localized infections become trapped within the hoof wall and sole, which can't expand to accommodate swelling. Severe pain can result.

A horse suffering from an acute abscess may hold up the affected leg as if it were broken. The key to healing abscesses is to locate and drain the built-up pus. Your farrier or veterinarian can use hoof-testers (big metal pincers) to pinpoint the infection site, then use a hoof knife to cut a channel through the sole to the abscess. This will reduce the pressure, providing immediate pain relief for your horse. Subsequent soaking and hoof poultices can facilitate a speedy recovery. (Ask your farrier, vet, or a knowledgeable horse person to show you how to soak and poultice a foot.)

Contracted Heels

Horses who have been improperly shod over time, who have naturally poor conformation, or who suffer from chronic soreness may develop this problem. The heels literally contract: shrink and narrow in size. Unlike round, bulbous healthy heels, they no longer provide maximum shock-absorbing and blood-circulating benefits. Over time, a good farrier may be able to improve this condition with proper shoeing.

Laminitis (or Founder) – See Chapter 22.

Navicular Disease

The navicular bone (another bone located inside the hoof) can also be a site for inflammation, usually caused by excessive concussion and/or poorly balanced hooves. Symptoms include mild to severe heel pain. As the disease progresses, the navicular bone gradually deteriorates, resulting in permanent soundness problems. Although some horses with navicular disease can be maintained with careful shoeing and judicious use of pain medications, those with severe cases often face early retirement.

Thrush

One of the surest signs of poor stable management is a frog (the v-shaped structure on the bottom of the hoof) oozing black, rotten-smelling gunk. This condition, known as "thrush," develops when opportunistic anaerobic bacteria in dirty, damp environments find their way into your horse's frogs. If the hooves remain packed with mud and dirt for an extended period of time, they create an oxygen-free environment in which the bacteria can thrive. Left unchecked, the infection works its way deep into the cleft of the frog, causing soreness and deterioration of the internal structures of the hoof.

Your first line of defense against thrush is simple: Keep the hooves clean and dry. If thrush does set in, you can kill the bacteria with various disinfectants, such as household bleach, hydrogen peroxide, turpentine, copper sulfate, or products made specifically to treat thrush. Ask your farrier or veterinarian to help you diagnose the condition and pick a suitable treatment.

Another reason to pick out your horse's feet daily is to check for anything suspicious—smells, cracks, loose shoes, etc.

Toe or Quarter (Side) Cracks

These can start at the coronary band and work their way down or start at the hoof surface and work their way up. Although cracks can be superficial and harmless at first, if allowed to spread, they can deepen and cause more serious problems. The best prevention against them is regular trimming and balancing.

Hoof-Care Products

All topical products and dietary supplements should be considered secondary defenses against hoof problems. Your number-one defenses are regular farrier visits, good stable management, and good basic nutrition.

If you think your horse needs a particular hoof-care product, consult with your farrier about his specific needs. For example, a horse with very dry hooves may benefit from a topical hoof dressing or moisturizer. On the opposite extreme, a weak hoof or one that's exposed to repeated damp/dry extremes may benefit from a "hoof hardener." "Polishes" are never recommended, as they interfere with the hoof's natural ability to regulate its internal moisture content.

A good diet usually provides all of the nutrients necessary for hoof-building and repair. In the case of nutrient deficiencies, however, a dietary supplement may help promote better growth. Unfortunately, because equine supplements aren't regulated, it's hard to ensure that the nutrients your horse needs are actually in the product. Ask your farrier to recommend a reputable brand. It will take several months before you notice any change in growth resulting from the supplement. It may also be difficult to prove that it was the supplement, rather than a change of season, exercise demands, or footing, that caused an improvement.

The Lowdown on Legs

Considering the tremendous weight they support and the high speeds they achieve, equine legs are remarkably delicate structures. It's a rare horse who lives his entire life without suffering from some form of leg injury. Factors influencing a horse's soundness include conformation (structural alignment and symmetry); concussion; nutrition; the quality of his conditioning program; and, last but not least, luck.

Some horses just seem to be luckier than others. The quality of care you provide can be a great influence, too. Unnoticed or untreated minor injuries can sometimes develop into serious, even permanent unsoundnesses, especially if you continue exercising your horse while he's injured.

Unfortunately, even veterinarians can't always pinpoint the cause of a subtle lameness. Whatever observations and information you can share with your veterinarian may help him or her solve the mystery.

Get to Know His Legs

The better you know your horse's legs, the faster you'll be able to identify and minimize problems. Start by spending a little time learning how they look and feel on a normal day. Tie, crosstie, or have a friend hold him in a well-lit area.

When you know your horse and how he normally moves, whether mounted or on his own, it's easy to tell if he's sore.

Then crouch down next to each leg (don't kneel or sit down—you won't be able to move out of his way fast enough if he suddenly spooks) and:

1. Visually examine the entire leg, familiarizing yourself with the normal angles, bumps, depressions, and scars.
2. Starting at the knee or hock, run your hand slowly down the leg, feeling the structures underneath the skin, noting where they feel hard and soft.
3. Repeat #2, this time feeling for changes in temperature in his legs and hooves. If you come across a particularly warm spot, feel the same area on the opposite leg to compare. You may have to go back and forth a few times to judge if they're the same temperature—which, ideally, they should be.
4. Finally, ask an experienced horse person to show you how to take the pulse in your horse's feet and palpate the tendons in his front legs. Both of these skills take a little more practice, but they can be invaluable later on.

Make a habit of checking your horse's legs, particularly after strenuous rides. Look for abnormal swelling, heat, sensitivity, cuts, or a strong pulse in a foot—all indicators of a brewing problem. Check again a few hours after the ride to see if things have changed. (Swelling may take an hour or two to show up after an injury.) Call your veterinarian if you notice anything out of the ordinary.

Is He Lame?

That question's often harder to answer than you think. A "head-bobbing" lame horse—one limping so dramatically that his head bobs up each time he puts weight on the sore foot—is pretty easy to spot. (If you're riding a horse who suddenly goes very lame, stop immediately and dismount. Check his hooves for an obvious injury, a thrown shoe, or a sharp rock stuck in his foot.) Unfortunately, many lamenesses are very subtle, showing up only on firm footing, on sharp turns, or as a horse is warming up. As you get to know your horse's

Believe it or not, horses have no muscles or fat in their lower legs. The bones (and hooves) below the knee and hock joints are manipulated by tendons and ligaments connected to muscles higher up in the legs.

normal way of going, you may be able to pick up slight changes in his gaits—shorter steps or stiffer movement. If you suspect that he may be lame, ask your instructor to watch him move or consult your veterinarian.

Stocking Up

Edema, or fluid build-up, in the lower legs, also called stocking up, happens to some horses, particularly older ones who've done a lot of training and competing, when they stand in a stall for a long period of time. The legs look fat and puffy and, when you press a finger into the skin, it leaves an indentation. Stocking up usually isn't painful and doesn't cause unsoundness. The swelling disappears during exercise or when the horse is turned out to pasture. It can be minimized by increasing your horse's turn-out time and applying stable/standing bandages to the legs when he's stabled.

Rest and relaxation may be all that's needed for your horse to recover from a leg problem, but your veterinarian needs to make that determination.

What's That Hitch in His Stride?

Some horses suffer from a gait impairment called "stringhalt," which causes an odd, abrupt, jerking motion of the hind leg. It's barely noticeable in some cases, but in others, it may look like the horse is trying to kick a fly off of his belly. The condition is believed to result from an extra nerve impulse sent to the leg from the spinal column. It causes no pain--and the horse may not even realize it's happening.

Stringhalt may be confused with three more serious conditions: upward fixation of the patella (hyperextension of the stifle joint), equine protozoal myeloencephalitis (EPM), and "shivers." Since these other problems can be more dangerous, ask your veterinarian to perform a full exam to determine exactly what your horse has.

Edema in the legs can be associated with many viral and bacterial infections, which may also cause fever. So, if your horse stocks up, check his temperature to be sure it's not a sign of something more serious.

Common Leg Ailments and Injuries

As you're first familiarizing yourself with your horse's legs, you may come across signs of past injuries. If these are cold and not making him lame, you probably have nothing to worry about. However, if they change over time—developing heat or swelling—that's a sign for concern.

Lumps and Bumps
Splints

These bony enlargements develop on the splint bones, which extend along either side of the top third of the cannon bone. They often develop in young horses starting training. Sometimes sensitive and causing lameness at first, splints usually heal on their own, calcifying (building up bony scar tissue) into hard knobs up to the size of a quarter.

Windpuff

Another harmless blemish, this soft, fluid-filled lump just above the fetlock joint rarely causes soreness or unsoundness.

Sidebones

These calcifications of cartilage just above the hairline on the outside of each hoof rarely cause problems.

Ringbone

Wear and tear between two of the pastern bones, an inch or so above your horse's coronary band, can cause arthritis in this joint. Ringbone is common in horses who do a lot of twisting and turning at speed: barrel racers, reiners, and upper-level dressage horses. As the condition progresses, it can cause chronic lameness.

"Big knee"

Normally, the fronts of your horse's knees should be fairly flat. If he's experienced some sort of trauma to them, though (hit a jump, slipped and fallen on his knees, etc.), he may develop puffy swelling as big as a softball. Even after the injury heals, the unsightly swelling may remain.

Bone and Bog Spavin

The hock joint—the elbow-shaped joint in the hind leg—is one of the main sites of unsoundness in performance horses. Bone spavin, the most common source of pain and lameness in the hind leg, occurs as a hard swelling on the lower, inside part of the joint. It can either result from osteochondrosis (OCD), a genetic growth problem in young horses, or repetitive stress in older horses. There are many treatments available for relieving symptoms (see below) but, as the disease progresses, chronic lameness is almost always unavoidable.

Trauma or OCD can cause bog spavin, a puffy swelling on the front or side of the upper part of the hock joint. Unlike bone spavin, bog spavin usually doesn't cause soundness problems after the initial injury resolves.

Thoroughpin

This is another puffy swelling that you may find in the back of your horse's hock, in the area between the point of the hock and the rest of the joint. There's usually a natural depression here, but it can be filled with a golf-ball-sized lump. Like bog spavin, thoroughpins usually don't cause lameness.

Capped Hock

Horses with the bad habit of kicking at their stall walls (for example, at feeding time) often develop unattractive lumps on the points of their hocks. These pockets of fluid result from direct trauma, but they generally don't cause soundness problems.

Sprains and Strains

The soft structures (tendons and ligaments) of your horse's lower legs can suffer various strains and sprains during the course of his career. The combination of sress and fatigue, sometimes in conjunction with other factors, such as poor conformation, hard or slippery footing, and unfortunate missteps, can

If your horse does need extra support for his legs, proper bandaging is critical. You need the right materials and the right technique.

lead to tendon and ligament injuries.

In racehorses, steeplechasers, and upper-level event horses, "bowed" tendons (severe tearing in the fibers of the deep or superficial flexor tendon) can be career-ending. Fortunately, "bows" that are treated immediately with complete rest, cold therapy (see below), and anti-inflammatory medication often heal well enough for a horse to go on to less stressful careers, such as show hunters and western pleasure riding.

Other common soft-structure injuries in performance horses include suspensory-ligament and check-ligament strains. They may cause lameness, swelling, heat, and/or pain. The earlier you detect these injuries and have your veterinarian treat them, the better your horse's chances are of making a full recovery.

Bone Breaks

Broken bones are rare in pleasure and low-level performance horses. However, they do happen occasionally in traumatic accidents, particularly in the pasture. (For instructions on how to handle these situations, see Chapter 24.)

In racing, minor bone damage, such as stress fractures, bone chips (in joints), and bucked shins (microdamage to the fronts of the cannon bones), can develop into more serious problems if the injured horse isn't given adequate rest and care. Ex-racehorses who go on to new careers may suffer periodic problems caused by old bone injuries. That's why x-raying for things such as bone chips in joints is recommended during a pre-purchase veterinary exam.

Caring for the Legs

Horse owners tend to overdo it when it comes to leg

care. You'll see people slathering herbal remedies, liniments, poultices, and other topical treatments on their horses' legs, then covering them up with bandages. Most of these treatments aren't necessary! More importantly, they can mask developing problems, increasing the risk of your unknowingly aggravating an injury by continuing to work your injured horse.

The best care you can give your horse's legs is the daily checkup described earlier in this chapter. If your horse has a particularly hard workout or you suspect that he's suffered an injury, wait at least two hours before treating the leg with a topical product and/or applying a bandage. It's much more important to identify a problem before blindly treating it. Give the leg time to tell you what's going on—via swelling or heat. Then call your veterinarian to discuss the next step.

Wrap it Right!

As mentioned earlier in this book, a poorly wrapped bandage can do more damage than good. Too tight, it can cut off circulation in the leg and cause permanent damage to the tendons. Too loose, it can shift or come undone, risking getting tangled up in your horse's legs.

Knowing how to apply a good "standing" or "stable" bandage properly is one of the best skills a horse person can learn. You may need to apply one in an emergency situation over a wound, to hold a poultice in place, or to protect your horse's legs from injury in the trailer. Be sure you have the right materials: thick cotton padding or "quilts" about 16 inches high and 30 to 40 inches long (available at tack stores and in catalogs), and long, somewhat stretchy stable or polo bandages with Velcro on one end. (Don't use a super-stretchy bandage, such as Vetrap®, for this purpose.)

Schedule an hour or so to learn bandaging technique from and practice with a knowledgeable horse person. Once she says you're getting it right, keep practicing. Applying good bandages consistently is much harder than it looks. So, repeat the technique until you're comfortable with it and satisfied with the results. Your horse will thank you later!

Rest and Cold Therapy

These are the two most invaluable treatments for leg injuries. As soon as you suspect a soundness problem, stop working your horse. Once your veterinarian has diagnosed the problem, allow your horse the full, prescribed rest period. The risk of re-injury is much higher if you start your horse back into work too soon or don't re-build his fitness and strength levels slowly enough.

Cold therapy does wonders for various injuries. Although inflammation is a normal part of the body's immune reaction to an injury, it can sometimes delay the healing process. Applying ice, mineral ice, or a steady stream of cold water from a hose ("cold hosing") in the first 24 hours after

Older horses with a lot of miles on them are prone to degenerative joint disease. A variety of treatments may help reduce their discomfort and prolong their careers.

an injury can be highly beneficial. Cold therapy may help relieve minor soreness and stiffness, as well.

Other Topical Treatments

You'll notice a wide variety of products on the market for various leg problems. In general, most of these are unnecessary. A well-planned conditioning program that doesn't cause aches and pains in the first place is much more important! However, if you do feel compelled to put something on your horse's legs, try an alcohol rub. Apply regular rubbing alcohol from the drug store or an alcohol gel (available through tack stores and catalogs) to his dry leg from the knee or hock down to his ankle. Gently massage it in with your hands, spending most of your energy on his ankles and the tendon area in the back of the lower leg. Be careful to keep the alcohol away from the coronary band and bulbs of his heels, where it can cause excessive drying.

Other topical treatments, such as poultices and liniments, have their place in leg care, as well. Ask an experienced horse person and/or your veterinarian to explain when and how to use them. Because liniment can cause mild irritation and heat in the tissues, never apply it to an open wound or an acute injury.

Arthritis Relief

If you put a lot of miles on your horse, at some time or another you're probably going to have to deal with degenerative joint disease, or arthritis—one of the most common leg ailments in performance horses. Like arthritis in humans, the flexible cartilage in your horse's joints is worn down slowly by repetitive motion, triggering swelling and pain. As the disease progresses, the cartilage and bones begin to change shape and deteriorate.

This irreversible process is hard to slow down. However, researchers and drug and neutraceutical companies are hard at work developing new treatments to delay the symptoms of arthritis. Here are some that your veterinarian may recommend trying:

Joint-support Supplements

Some research indicates that these supplements at least provide short-term pain relief for arthritis sufferers. Claims that manufacturers make about longer-term effects, such as increases in joint fluid and cartilage repair, are still debatable. Because these products aren't regulated, do as much research as you can about the listed ingredients and the company's reputation for quality control.

Intra-articular (Joint) Injections

These shots are typically of anti-inflammatory medications such as corticosteroids or hyaluronic acid. Any time you stick a needle into the sterile capsule around a joint, you risk introducing bacteria that could contribute to serious infection. However, joint injections have prolonged the careers of many performance horses. Only qualified veterinarians should administer them.

Intramuscular (IM) Injections

Regular administration of systemic joint-health medications, such as Legend® and Adequan®, may increase the lubrication and decrease the swelling within an arthritic joint.

NSAIDs

Phenylbutazone, or "bute," is one of the most common non-steroidal anti-inflammatory drugs in the horse industry. Short-term use for pain relief and swelling reduction can be highly effective, but long-term use can contribute to liver and kidney problems. Some animals, particularly ponies and foals, are susceptible to potentially fatal bute toxicity. So be judicious with your bute use and consult your veterinarian about safer alternative treatments.

Chapter 24

Equine First Aid

Because horses are flight animals, they often "run first, ask questions later." When this happens, they will sometimes crash their bodies into walls and other obstacles, incurring sometimes severe injuries. Horse-related accidents can happen anywhere: in the barn, on the trail, in the trailer, at shows, etc. Here's how to handle them.

Steps to Take in an Emergency: Don't Panic!

The last thing a terrified, hurting horse needs is a hysterical owner. Whatever the situation, stay calm and speak to your horse in a low, soothing voice. Make your safety your top priority. If he's panicking in a tight space or thrashing dangerously, don't approach him. Instead, go get help from an experienced horse person. If your horse is trapped—in a crumpled trailer after an accident, in a ditch on the trail, etc., call your local fire department for help.

Restrain Your Horse

Tie him in a safe place or ask a friend to hold him. If he's too hurt to move, ask a friend to call the veterinarian while you stay to keep him quiet and still.

Evaluate the Situation

Make a swift examination of your horse and his surroundings. Ask yourself the following questions: Is he injured? If so, how badly? Is there more than one wound? (You may miss another serious injury if you zero in right away on the first one you notice.) Can he be treated safely where he is or does he have to be moved? Are there any obviously broken bones? Are the injuries major enough to require veterinary attention?

You may be able to treat mild scrapes and shallow cuts on your own. However, if the injury involves his eyes or a joint, or if it appears to be a puncture wound, but you can't tell how deep it is, it may be more serious than it looks. When in doubt, call the vet.

Stop the Bleeding

Horses have a lot of blood in their bodies, so a large amount of lost blood may not be as life-threatening as it'd be for a human. However, too much blood loss can lead to shock and even death. It's especially important to stem the flow of blood that's pulsing (indicating a nicked artery or vein) or streaming out of a wound. Use a sterile non-stick pad or a clean towel to press against the wound. If the wound is on the leg, wrap Vetrap® around the area to keep the pad in place or cover it with a tight standing bandage. Otherwise, hold the pad in place with your hand for at least five minutes.

If the wound is not pulsing or bleeding heavily, leave it alone until the veterinarian arrives. Don't put any topical ointments on it or give your horse any medications unless he or she advises you to do so. If a foreign object is stuck in the wound, leave it in place until the veterinarian arrives.

Check Vital Signs

Take your horse's pulse, respiratory rate, and temperature, and evaluate his mucus membranes (see Chapter 21).

Call the Veterinarian

Be prepared to give your veterinarian a full history of recent events. Be honest about your own skills, too. If he or she asks if you know how to apply a pressure bandage and you don't, say so. In dire emergencies, your veterinarian may be able to talk you through certain procedures over the phone. Otherwise, your answers will help in deciding how quickly he or she needs to attend to your horse in person.

An overheated horse will need plenty of fresh water.

If your horse is injured on the road or in a location beyond your regular vet's practice, call 911. The police should be able to get you in touch with a local veterinarian.

Mild Wounds

For mild scrapes and abrasions that don't completely disrupt the skin and tissues underneath, follow these guidelines:

1. Rinse the cut clean with a steady, gentle stream of water.
2. Fill a small, clean bucket with warm water. Soak a handful of sterile cotton in the water and then pour antiseptic liquid (like Betadine) liberally onto it. Gently cleanse the wound and rinse it thoroughly with warm water.
3. Dry the wound with sterile gauze pads, and then dry the surrounding skin with a clean towel.
4. If your veterinarian recommends applying a topical wound ointment, apply this to the clean cut.
5. Finally, if the wound is on an area of the leg that can be bandaged, and you have good bandaging skills, cover the wound with a nonstick sterile pad and wrap it in place with a thickly padded stable bandage. Change the bandage twice daily until the wound stops draining and starts to heal. As soon as a scab has formed, stop bandaging altogether.
6. If the wound is in an area that can't be bandaged and it's bug season, apply a fly-repellant ointment made specifically for wounds.
7. Meanwhile, if the wound is in an area that experiences a lot of motion (the knee or shoulder, for instance), confine your horse to a stall or try to keep him quiet otherwise, so as to prevent re-opening the wound as it heals.
8. Most importantly, try to discover the cause of every injury. Check your horse's stall and pasture for sharp objects, damaged fencing, or anything else he may have run into. If you suspect that another horse kicked him, consider separating them in the future.

Eye Injuries

If your horse has an obvious eye injury or if you notice symptoms of the eye problems described in Chapter 22, apply a triple-antibiotic ophthalmic ointment immediately and call your veterinarian. (Ask for a tube of this medication to keep in your first-aid kit, and for instructions on how to administer it.)

Choke

Horses don't choke on food the same way humans do. Instead of getting food stuck in their windpipes, risking cutting off their breathing, they experience obstructions in the esophagus (the tube food and water go through to get from the mouth to the stomach). If the obstruction isn't removed within a few hours, it can cause lasting damage to the esophagus. Also, an obstruction can cause food to pile up in the esophagus, causing your horse to "aspirate" (breathe in saliva). This can lead to serious pneumonia.

Horses suffering from choke usually stand still in their stalls, neither eating nor drinking, with large amounts of slimy, green discharge (mixed in with food particles) coming out of their noses. They may also display obvious signs of discomfort, such as pawing and coughing—or may have a panicked expression in their faces. If you notice any of these signs, call your veterinarian immediately.

The condition can be caused by a horse eating too quickly ("bolting" his food) or not chewing his food sufficiently. This can be especially dangerous with pelleted grain or unsoaked beet pulp, both of which will swell when moistened by saliva. To prevent your horse from "bolting" his feed, put a few softball-sized rocks or bricks in his feed tub. Also consider switching to a non-pelleted feed—and toss him plenty of hay in between meals so he's not starving at mealtime.

Coming to the Rescue!

Some volunteer fire departments include equine/large-animal rescue units that train rescuers to safely extricate horses from ravines, ditches, collapsed barns, overturned trailers, etc. With specially designed slings, harnesses and pulley systems, used in conjunction with tractors, cranes, and even helicopters, these equine saviors can lift horses off the ground and transport them to safety.

Many fire and police departments, search-and-rescue units, and other groups practice safe rescue and immobilization techniques with "Lucky," a life-sized equine mannequin that stands 15 hands tall and weighs 400 pounds (about half the weight of an average horse). Lucky has jointed, movable limbs and realistic tail and head features.

Chapter 25

Alternative Medicine and High-Tech Therapies

Equine medicine is heading in two exciting new directions. First, it's following the recent trend in human medicine toward accepting alternative therapies, such as chiropractic, homeopathy, herbology/naturopathy, and acupuncture. (Since many of these therapies have been used for centuries in Eastern medicine, not everybody sees them as alternative.)

*A*t the same time, traditional veterinary medicine is becoming more and more high-tech, offering horse owners sophisticated, comprehensive tools to diagnose and treat everything ranging from subtle lameness to chronic arthritis. In general, the newer the technique, the more money it'll cost you. (Many high-tech treatments were first developed to treat expensive racehorses and sport horses.) However, as these treatments turn mainstream, they'll become more affordable for the average horse owner, too.

Alternative Medicine

The most important thing to remember about alternative medicine is that many of its techniques have less research behind them than more conventional therapies. That doesn't mean they don't work; it just means that, until more research is done, they shouldn't be your primary line of defense against equine health problems, particularly serious ones like broken legs, colic, and deep wounds.

If you do your research, though, and find a veterinary practitioner trained in these techniques, you can use them to complement your horse's basic traditional care. Before hiring an alternative therapist to work on your horse, first check that he or she is certified by a respected national organization, licensed to practice in your state, and recommended by people who have used his or her services (your veterinarian, trainer, friends, etc.).

Acupuncture

Equine acupuncture is used to treat a variety of problems, including arthritis, navicular disease, back and neck pain, respiratory problems, colic, and many other conditions. Today's treatments may attach mild electric currents to the needles, use heated needles, or inject liquids, such as B vitamins, to further stimulate parts of the nervous system. Manual pressure ("acupressure") or laser treatment may be used instead of needles.

Chiropractic

This is the form of alternative medicine that can be most dangerous if done improperly, so be scrupulous in your choice of practitioner and closely watch how he or she works. If you have any fear that the techniques being performed on your horse may cause an injury—and some improper techniques can—politely ask the practitioner to stop working on your horse.

Many behavioral or training problems such as bucking, rearing, difficulty taking one canter lead or changing leads, and "girthiness" (showing irritation when the girth or cinch is being tightened) can be caused by a misalignment in the neck, back, or pelvis. Other symptoms include stiffness and subtle, difficult-to-locate lameness. Having more trouble doing something in one direction than the other is also a common indication of poor alignment.

Good chiropractic treatment can help address these problems by increasing range of motion, promoting joint health, and helping to prevent further injuries. It can't, however, reverse severe joint damage, such as degenerative arthritis. If your horse is suffering from a fresh wound or may have a bone fracture, this is not the time for chiropractic treatment, either. Call your veterinarian first in any emergency situation.

Herbology/Naturopathy

One of the most dangerously misunderstood concepts of alternative medicine is that "natural" treatments, such as plant- and herb-based oral supplements, are safe. Many are but, unless their labels make specific claims about their intended uses, "natural" products don't have to go through the rigorous safety and efficacy tests that drugs go through. Some herbs can actually be toxic, even in small amounts

The Carrot Trick

Does your horse need a chiropractor? One way to find out is to test his flexibility with the "carrot trick." Stand by his hip and offer him a carrot or some other treat to lure his head to the back and side. A normal horse should be able to reach his nose to his hip. If your horse has to duck his head or can't reach very far back, his neck or back may be restricted. Test him on both sides to see if he's better on one side than the other.

Next, stand by his shoulder and hold a carrot between his front legs to draw his head down. He should be able to reach his nose between his knees. Again, if he can't, that's a sign of restriction in his neck and back. Whether or not you call the chiropractor, these are still great stretches to do regularly with your horse. Try to make it very clear that he only gets the treat when he does the stretch. That way, he's less likely to start bugging and nipping at you for treats.

Just like human athletes, sport horses benefit from comprehensive wellness programs that incorporate alternative and high-tech, as well as traditional, medicine.

(Remember Socrates? He died after eating hemlock—a "natural" plant!)

Not all herbs work the same in horses and humans, either. So do your research: Find books on herbs, research them on the Internet, and consult experts with both human herbal training and knowledge of equine physiology.

Homeopathy

Unlike herbs and traditional medicines, homeopathy functions under the premise of "like cures like." Minute quantities of animal-, vegetable-, or mineral-derived remedies that might be toxic in larger doses are used to trigger an immune response in the body, somewhat the way vaccines use small amounts of live or killed virus to build up the body's defenses against a disease. The recommended potency of homeopathic remedies, "30C," is very safe and shouldn't cause any ill reactions or side effects in your horse.

One of the most commonly used homeopathic remedies in the equine world is arnica. It's often used to treat muscle strain, soreness, and bruising. Like other homeopathic remedies, it can be dissolved in water (four to five 30C pellets in 12cc of water) and injected directly into your horse's mouth with a syringe, or applied topically in a liquid or cream form.

Always consult your veterinarian before trying any herb on your horse. If you plan to compete with him, check with your veterinarian and your sport association to be sure the herb is legal. Some herbs test positive on drugs tests, and can get you eliminated from competition.

Because homeopathic remedies are so specific, you may need to try several different ones before finding the right solution for a particular problem. As with any other alternative medicine, however, always consult your veterinarian first about any serious conditions or injuries.

High-Tech Therapies

Scanning/Diagnostic Techniques

Until not long ago, x-rays, ultrasound, and endoscopes were the highest-tech diagnostic tools used in equine medicine. The latest imaging tools now include:

Thermography

A non-invasive method that shows changes in blood flow in the body, indicating areas of acute pain and inflammation or chronic pain

Nuclear scintigraphy (or bone scanning)

Uses a radioactive isotope (administered to the horse beforehand) to identify areas where the bone is more metabolically active; i.e., where the body is working to repair damage

Fluoroscopy

Using this hand-held video camera, veterinarians can create a 360-degree view of a bone structure or joint, rather than having to take a series of x-rays from many different angles.

If you enjoy petting and nuzzling your horse, you can easily take it one step further and turn your touch into therapeutic massage.

Therapeutic Techniques

Laser Therapy

Different from the powerful cutting lasers used in human and equine surgery techniques, devices used for this therapy are "cold" lasers or light-emitting diodes (LEDs), which provide "photon therapy." This can be focused on an injury site to reduce inflammation and speed healing, used to boost the immune system, and used with acupuncture for horses who don't like needles.

Electromagnetic Therapy

Pulsed electromagnets (magnets powered with electricity) can be applied in various types of bandages and blankets to most parts of the horse's body. The exact mechanism and benefit of the therapy is still debatable, but many people believe it increases metabolism and speeds healing.

Ultrasound Therapy

Therapeutic ultrasound emits powerful sound waves that create friction in living tissue, producing heat at a very deep level, without elevating the skin-surface temperature. It can penetrate deep body structures such as joints, tendons, and thick muscles, increasing metabolic activity and blood flow to facilitate healing. Because improper use of the device can damage deep tissues, it's very important to have a qualified veterinarian or physical therapist apply the treatment.

Extracorporeal Shock-Wave Therapy (ESWT or lithotripsy)

This therapy uses high-energy shock waves to stimulate healing in bone and joint-related problems. It isn't painless, so horses need to be sedated during treatment.

Massage

This therapy falls somewhere in between the alternative and high-tech camps—and it is generally accepted by proponents of both. Just as with human massage, equine massage can loosen tight muscles, increasing range of motion and blood circulation. As a result, your horse's strides lengthen, his power, endurance, coordination, and reflexes improve, and you lower his risk of injury.

Many well-educated, skilled, experienced, sports-massage therapists are trained to work specifically on horses. Look for a practitioner who has extensive training, preferably a full-human massage course as well as equine training.

You may want to try to massage your horse yourself. Pick the largest muscles over his shoulders, back, and hindquarters. Using the heel of one hand or a loose fist, press and release on the belly (the thick center) of the muscle, in a rhythmic one-two motion. Start at the highest point of the muscle belly and work your way down it. You should feel tighter muscles soften under your hands as you work. On thicker muscles, you can press fairly hard. On thinner muscles covering bone (such as the shoulder area), be gentler. Watch your horse's expression to judge if you're using too little or too much pressure.

Although many horses love massage, the occasional touchy horse will react negatively to it. If your horse shows any sign of biting or kicking, stop treatment immediately. Also stay clear of sensitive areas, such as the flanks, if you know your horse doesn't like being touched there.

Educational Organizations

The American Horse Council
1616 H Street, NW
Washington, DC 20006-3805
202-296-4031
www.horsecouncil.org

American Riding Instructors Association
28801 Trenton Ct.
Bonita Springs, FL 34134-3337
239-948-3232
www.riding-instructor.com

The British Horse Society
Stoneleigh Deer Park
Stareton Lane
Kenilworth, Warwickshire
CV8 2XZ England
www.bhs.org.uk

Canadian 4-H Council
930 Carling Avenue
Ottawa, Ontario
K1A 0C6 Canada
www.4-h-canada.ca

Canadian Pony Club
CPC National Office
Box 127
Baldur, MB R0K 0B0
Canada
www.canadianponyclub.org

Centered Riding, Inc
P.O. Box 12377
Philadelphia, PA 19119
215-438-1286
www.centeredriding.org

Equine Canada
2460 Lancaster Rd.
Ottawa, Ontario K1B 4S5
Canada
613-248-3433
www.equinecanada.ca

National 4-H Council
7100 Connecticut Ave.
Chevy Chase, MD 20815-4999
301-961-2959
www.fourhcouncil.edu

The Pony Club (UK)
Stoneleigh Park
Kenilworth
Warwickshire
CV8 2RW England
www.pcuk.org

United States Equestrian Federation
The National Governing Body for Equestrian Sports
4047 Iron Works Parkway
Lexington, KY 40511
859-258-2472
www.usef.com

United States Pony Clubs, Inc.
4041 Iron Works Parkway
Lexington, KY 40511
859-254-7669
www.ponyclub.org

Publications

Arabian Horse World
656 Quince Orchard Rd. #600
Gaithersburg, MD 20878-1472
301-977-3900
www.equisearch.com

Chronicle of the Horse
P.O. Box 46
Middleburg, VA 20018
540-687-6341
www.chronofhorse.com

Dressage Today
656 Quince Orchard Rd. #600
Gaithersburg, MD 20878-1472
301-977-3900
www.equisearch.com

Endurance News
American Endurance Riding Conference
P.O. Box 6027
Auburn, CA 95604
530-823-2260
www.aerc.org

Equestrian
United States Equestrian Federation
4047 Iron Works Parkway
Lexington, KY 40511
859-258-2472
www.usef.com

Equus
656 Quince Orchard Rd. #600
Gaithersburg, MD 20878-1472
301-977-3900
www.equisearch.com

Horse & Rider
656 Quince Orchard Rd. #600
Gaithersburg, MD 20878-1472
301-977-3900
www.equisearch.com

Horse Connection
380 Perry Street, #210
Castle Rock, CO 80104
303-663-1300
www.horseconnection.com

Horse Illustrated
P.O. Box 6050
Mission Viejo, CA 92690
949-855-8822
www.horseillustratedmagazine.com

Practical Horseman
656 Quince Orchard Rd. #600
Gaithersburg, MD 20878-1472
301-977-3900
www.equisearch.com

Thoroughbred Times
P.O. Box 8237
496 Southland Dr.
Lexington, KY 40533-8237
www.thoroughbredtimes.com

USDF Connections
United States Dressage Federation
220 Lexington Green Circle
Lexington, KY 40503
859-971-2277
www.usdf.org

Western Horseman
P.O. Box 7980
Colorado Springs, CO 80933-7980
719-633-5524
www.westernhorseman.com

Equine Sport Organizations

American Driving Society
P.O. Box 160
Metamora, MI 48455-0160
810-664-8666
www.americandrivingsociety.org

American Endurance Riding Conference
P.O. Box 6027
Auburn, CA 95604
530-823-2260
www.aerc.org

American Hunter and Jumper Foundation
335 Lancaster Street
P.O. Box 369
West Boylston, MA 01583

American Vaulting Association
642 Alford Place
Bainbridge Island, WA 98110-3657
206-780-9353
www.americanvaulting.org

Canadian Sport Horse Association
P.O. Box 1625
Holland Landing, Ontario
L9N 1P2 Canada
905-830-9288
www.canadian-sport-horse-org

Federation Equestre International
Avenue Mon-Repos 24
P.O. Box 157
CH-1000 Lausanne 5 Switzerland
www.horsesport.org

National Barrel Horse Association
725 Broad Street
P.O. Box 1988
Augusta, GA 30903-1988
706-722-7223
www.nbha.com

National Cutting Horse Association
4704 Highway 377 S.
Fort Worth, TX 76116-8805
817-244-6188
www.nchacutting.com

National Steeplechase Association
400 Fair Hill Drive
Elkton, MD 21921
410-392-0700
www.nationalsteeplechase.com

North American Riding for the Handicapped Association
P.O. Box 33150
Denver, CO 80233
303-452-1212
www.narha.org

United States Combined Training Association
525 Old Waterford Rd, NW
Leesburg, VA 20176-2050
703-779-0440
www.eventingusa.com

United States Dressage Federation
220 Lexington Green Circle
Lexington, KY 40503
859-971-2277
www.usdf.org

United States Equestrian Team
1040 Pottersville Road
P.O. Box 355
Gladstone, NJ 07934-9955
908-234-1251
www.uset.org

Veterinary Organizations

American Association of Equine Practitioners
4075 Iron Works Parkway
Lexington, KY 40511
www.myhorsematters.com

American Veterinary Medical Association
1931 North Meacham Road - Suite 100
Schaumburg, IL 60173
847-925-8070
www.avma.org

British Equine Veterinary Association
Wakefield House
46 High Street
Sawston, Cambridgeshire
CB2 4BG England
www.beva.org.uk

Canadian Veterinary Medical Association
339 Booth Street
Ottawa, ON
K1R 7K1
Canada
613-236-1162
www.canadianveterinarians.net

Equine Welfare Organizations

The Fund for Horses
914 Dallas, #403
Houston, TX 77002
713-650-1973
www.fund4horses.org

International League for the Protection of Horses
Anne Colvin House
Snetterton Norfolk
NR16 2LR England
www.ilph.org

National Horse Protection Coalition
P.O. Box 1252
Alexandria, VA 22313
www.horse-protection.org

Thoroughbred Retirement Foundation
PMB 351, 450 Shrewsbury Plaza
Shrewsbury, NJ 07702-4332
732-957-0182
www.trfinc.org

Index

Note: **Boldface** numbers indicate illustrations.

Index